THEORY OF INDIAN MUSIC

THEORY OF INDIAN MUSIC

RAI BAHADUR BISHAN SWARUP

GYAN

Published by

Gyan Publishing House
5, Ansari Road
Daryaganj, New Delhi-110002
Phone: 011-47034999, 9811692060
E-mail: books@gyanbooks.com

Distribution Network
gyanbooks.com
India, USA, Canada, UK, Australia

ISBN: 978-93-7414-132-8 (HB)

First Published, 1933

2nd Impression 2026

Printed at: Gyan Press, Delhi.

THEORY OF INDIAN MUSIC
Author: RAI BAHADUR BISHAN SWARUP

THEORY

OF

INDIAN MUSIC

BY

RAI BAHADUR BISHAN SWARUP
RETIRED CHIEF ENGINEER AND SECRETARY
TO THE GOVERNMENT OF B. & O.

SWARUP BROTHERS
MAITHAN AGRA

—

1933

PREFACE

WHEN the Senate of the Patna University, of which I had the honour to be a member, passed the introduction of music in the University, one of the subjects prescribed was the theory of Indian music It was then that I thought of writing a book on the subject, although I could not make a beginning until long after my retirement five years ago I did not realise at the time that it was such a difficult task, there being hardly any Indian book available that dealt with the subject scientifically, not that the broad principles of Indian music are not known to the present day music experts, or not found in any of the books, but how these principles came into existence, or why it is necessary to follow them is not to be found anywhere Shrutis and Gramas, for instance, are common terms in Indian music, but I have not seen a single book explaining clearly and correctly what is meant by those terms. An endeavour has been made in these pages to get at how the several principles governing Indian music came to be established and it is a matter of gratification to find that all of them have scientific bases

The chief function of music, the expression of sentiments, as also the psychological interpretation of tunes, is altogether absent from the books on Indian music. Sharngdeva in his *Sangita Ratnakara* no doubt mentions the sentiments expressed by the tunes of his time, but that cannot be of any use to us, as the tunes, being some 700 years old, are all obsolete, and the method of interpretation has not been explained.

The art of harmony, which it is universally and perhaps rightly said does not exist in Indian music, but which was practised in old times as has been shown in this book, does not find even a mention in any of the books available.

All this required original investigation, and a treatment of the subject altogether different from that found in the existing treatises. An attempt has, however, been made to explain the subjects dealt with as lucidly and clearly as possible, giving illustrations where necessary.

I fully realise the imperfectness of the production, partly due to the subject being altogether new, but mostly to my own shortcomings All that is hoped is that it will create a deserved respect for the principles laid down by the ancient writers, give a start to their scientific application and provide material for further investigation

B SWARUP

CONTENTS

CONTENTS.

CONTENTS

CONTENTS.

THEORY OF INDIAN MUSIC

Chapter I

INTRODUCTION

Music a Fine Art Comparison with other Fine Arts Music in India separated from Poetry Subjects included in Music

THE Indian word for music is Sangíta, which means a chorus or a song sung by many voices, and also applies to singing accompanied by playing of instruments and dancing In its vast compass, therefore Indian music includes music in all its forms, vocal, instrumental, choral, together with the allied arts of dancing and gesticulating As in all other advanced countries so in India, music is considered to be a fine art As such it may be defined as an art which employs sounds (not necessarily words), combined so as to be agreeable to the ear, as a medium of expressing one's emotions and perceptions, and of creating in the hearers the emotions and perceptions desired by the artist It is the finest among the fine arts. A music artist has a more difficult task to perform than the other artists, sculptors, painters, poets and architects, because, while the latter present their work to the audience in a tangible shape with feelings expressed, the musician has to stimulate the imagination of his audience and thereby engender in them those feelings to make himself understood. The scene of a lady wailing over the long absence of her lover, for instance, when presented by a sculptor, or a painter, or a poet, can easily produce the desired effect, but it is not so easy to do so by means of mere tunes. This is owing to sculpture and painting being perceived through the eye, unlike music, which is perceived through the ear

Perceptions, we know, are transformed into emotions through ideas, based on previous experience, which require words to form them, and words have a much closer psychological connection with objects perceived by the eye than with those perceived by the ear A figure or a picture of the lady, or the mere words "lady wailing over the long absence of her lover", will create the desired emotions in the audience much sooner than the tune Bhúpálí, the appropriate tune to express and create those emotions, as it has first to excite the imagination of the audience to perceive the wailing of the lady, before any ideas can be formed and the desired emotion produced The name of the tune, *viz*, "Bhupálí", will not create any impression even in the audience who know the tune, but if a description of the tune is given, it will have some effect as it brings the scene before the mental vision The Rágini (tune) Bhupálí is described as a lady separated from her lover, wearing a yellow sárí (cloth) all her body turned pale due to the fire of separation

Music, being perceptible through the ear, thus takes time to have its effect on emotions, and it must be admitted that the emotions created are not very definite The help of words in the form of songs or poetry is therefore sought and acting is resorted to for better effect The whole history of European music is a history of composition of appropriate songs for different occasions, rather than the evolution of tunes The tunes were kept subordinated to the latter The tunes by themselves do not, and it was never perhaps meant that they should, produce partic ular emotions, and as such lose the character of a fine art.

In India the case has been different Here music was treated quite independently of poetry or songs. At the start when, for instance, the hymns of Sámaveda were sung over three thousand years ago, the tunes must have been composed to correspond with the subject-matter of the songs, and, *vice versa*, songs composed to describe what the tunes expressed Later, however, music was considered as a subject distinct from poetry.

This gave both an advantage and a disadvantage to the Indian music. The advantage was that it enabled the various notes to be clearly distinguished from one another; their relations to each other found out, their effect, severally, as well as in combination, on the human mind determined, in short, it enabled details being worked out on a scientific basis All this, and perhaps more, is to be found now in the European music also, but the credit of the scientific analysis must be given to the ancients, and India can easily claim to be the foremost among them

This scientific treatment of music, as a subject distinct from poetry, enabled the Indians to compose, by suitable combinations, a variety of tunes, some to express particular feelings and stimulate particular emotions, some for devotional purposes, some soothing to the brain and pleasing to the ear and so on, suitable for different hours of the day or different seasons of the year Each of these tunes excepting perhaps some recent combinations has been allotted a name, and can be distinguished by trained ears from others A good Indian musician can sing any song in any of the tunes, and so can select his tune for his songs to suit the particular occasion or the time of the day This is a great advantage, calculated to make music effective

The disadvantage of alienating music from poetry has been that tunes not having been fixed for the particular pieces of poetry or songs, the latter are not infrequently sung in tunes quite inappropriate to their subjects One sometimes hears songs with subjects like complaints against the frolicsome behaviour of Krishna made by the Gopikás of Gokul to his mother, sung in highly plaintive tunes like Sohiní Many good musicians not of course artists, are found offenders in this respect; nor are the Hindustani theatres altogether free from this defect Sometimes it is very jarring on the ear when a song is unsuited to the subject. To enjoy music, therefore, it is best, in such cases not to try to understand the subject of the song

The Indian poetry abounds in songs on all subjects, and also there are hundreds of tunes so that any feeling can be adequately expressed, but it is a matter of regret that the proper application is wanting In fact, leaving out the effort made of a revival in recent years, the use of music as a fine art seems to have been lost.

Reverting to the comparison between music and other fine arts, we have seen that, in the matter of expression, music has to exert itself much more for being effective than the other fine arts Music has, besides, other disadvantages While the other fine arts have prototypes in nature to copy, music has practically none readily available For a sculpture or a painting every phase of emotions can be found in everyday life. Poetry has words by which to express itself But in the case of music, it means evolving of principles by carefully considering the effect of each note and combination of notes.

Many of the human emotions are, no doubt, expressible by variations in tone of the voice, but those are difficult to catch and, until very recently, they could not be definitely recorded The subject was, notwithstanding the difficulty, thoroughly gone into, and as has been said above, Indian music possesses tunes representing almost every phase of human emotions As a matter of fact, this subject formed one of the seven parts of the books on Sangíta The seven parts, called "Adhyáyas" are (1) Surádhyáya, dealing with different notes, (2) Rágádhyáya, dealing with tunes, (3) Táladhyáya dealing with rhythm and timing, (4) Hastadhyaya dealing with the playing on instruments, (5) Nrityadhyaya on dancing, (6) Bhavadhyáya on gesticulating and acting and (7) Arthádhyáya on the meaning, sense and significa tion of the tunes The last part dealt with the subject

Leaving aside the question of expression and producing emotions, if we consider only the quality of exciting pleasure, or cheering one up when one feels miserable, music surpasses all other fine arts The latter do not even come near music in this respect The finest sculpture or painting would be passed scantily noticed, except by persons specially interested in those arts. On the contrary, any piece of music, vocal or instrumental, draws some sort of audience, the number and the nature of the hearers depending on the quality of the music. Its attractiveness may be seen from the fact that almost every entertainment has music of some sort on its programme.

Music, it has been observed, has its effect also upon lower animals. In India, the charming of snakes by playing on flutes (known as Bín) is a frequent experience. It is also said antelopes used to be caught by charming them with music. D'Israeli, in his "Curiosities of Literature", has given several anecdotes describing the effect of music on animals, which show how horses, dogs, hinds, mice, some of the birds, lizards, and even spiders, come out of their way to hear music.

The result of a musical experiment made in the London Zoo, described by the Director of the Zoo Society's Aquarium, may be interesting. He says (*vide* the ' Daily Telegraph" copied in the "Englishman" of 25th April, 1927) " The rhinoceros was found to have no ear for music, and attempted to charge the orchestra, no matter what tune was played

The sea lions on the other hand, were delighted with everything put before them with the exception of "jazz" No matter how busy playing in their pond, they paused, and rose to the surface as soon as the orchestra struck up Most of the melodies that had exasperated the rhino delighted them, and they remained standing waist-high out of the water until the last strains had died away

Thunder storms and war time gunfire have no effect upon the sea lions, so that mere noise cannot offer an explanation for enthusiasm The Zoo's wolves and jackals responded all too readily to the music offered A tune set in a minor key at once caused them to point their noses to the sky and give voice in so vociferous a manner as to drown completely the orchestra The minor key, depressing at all times, had a like effect upon most of the animals The cheetah thoroughly enjoyed "I want to be happy," but registered discontent and even alarm when favoured with Gounod's "Funeral March" The orchestra when playing in the reptile house never failed to bring the crocodile to the surface In fact every pond was emptied the beasts clustering on the banks and, with heads upraised, evincing the keenest interest in the performance. In the insect house, the like effect was obtained with the scorpions and certain spiders All birds, strange to say, were in no way attracted. Some were obviously annoyed."

Music is also said to possess medicinal properties. It is particularly effective in soothing the brain and many a disease of the brain has been cured by appropriate music It is also said to cure some nervous and other diseases, but it is doubtful if music can claim as much

Chapter II

SOUND

Sound-vibrations Musical sound, Pitch

Concordant sounds Octave Saptaka Sthana

MUSIC has been defined as an art of combining sounds in such a way as to be agreeable to the ear Sound is generated by the vibratory motion of the particles of a body caused by its getting into a state of tremor due to any shock or otherwise It is conveyed to the ear through an elastic medium such as air or water If a bell is rung inside a jar from which air has been extracted by means of an air pump, the sound of the bell cannot be heard, so a medium is necessary for hearing a sound The vibrations may be generated in the medium itself, as in the case of a flute In all cases, the vibrations are transmitted to the air (or other media) causing undulations, known as accoustic waves, which in turn cause vibrations in the membranes of the ear These stimulate the auditory nerves, which conduct the sound impulses to the brain, and make the sound heard

When a series of vibrations enters the ear at equal intervals of time, rapidly following each other, so that no intermission is perceived, the result is a musical sound. If the intervals are so long that the perception of a vibration is lost before the successive one is perceived, or if they are so short that the vibrations cannot be distinctly perceived, the sound ceases to have a musical character In the one case it will hardly be audible, in the other it will form a noise The minimum and maximum number of vibrations for the sounds which can be called musical are 16 and 8192 per second respectively Musical sounds, so far as their effect on the ear is concerned, are distinguished from each other by what are called their pitch, loudness and timbre

Pitch is what makes the sounds known as acute, shrill, high, sharp, grave, deep, low, flat, etc It depends on the rapidity of vibrations of the particles of the air in contact with the ear A low number of vibrations in a given time (say a second) gives grave or low tones, a high number giving acute or shrill tones; and the higher the number of vibrations, the shriller the tone Pitch is thus directly proportional to the number of vibrations.

Loudness depends on the violence with which the membranes of the ear are excited, and therefore on the extent or amplitude of the vibrations of the body *emitting the sound*

Timbre is the peculiarity of impression produced on the ear by the tone or sound of the instrument or voice which distinguishes it from a like tone or sound of another instrument or voice It depends on the harmonics co existing with the fundamental tone and their relative intensities The terms, harmonics and fundamental, will be defined further on

Of the three features of sound, pitch is by far the most important Several instruments have been designed to measure the pitch or the number of vibrations producing a sound The most simple and convenient comparative measure of the pitch is a string stretched over two supports, as in a Sitár or Víná On being struck, the string vibrates and produces sound, the number of vibrations depending on the density and thickness of the string the tension *with which it is stretched, and the distance* between the two supports The lighter the material is, the more tensely it is stretched, and the smaller the distance between the supports, the greater will be the number of vibrations in a given time and *vice versa* Supposing that the material of the string and the tension in it are uniform, and that the distance between the supports can be altered at will, the number of vibrations produced by striking the string will be inversely proportional to the length; half the length would give double the number of vibrations, one-third the length three times the number of vibrations, and so on

The notes of different pitch following each other or sounding together are more or less pleasing to the ear according to the frequency of coincidences of their vibrations in a given time. Supposing, for instance, four notes, P, Q, R, and S, have 400, 500, 600, and 800, vibrations per second respectively. Then in each second, the vibrations of P and Q coincide 100 times, of Q and R also 100 times, those of P and R coincide 200 times, and of P and S 400 times. The combination of P and R will be more pleasing than that of P and Q The relation of P and S is, except for the difference of pitch, the same as would have been with P and another note having 400 vibrations per second. Hence it is said that a note having double the number of vibrations in another note is the same as the latter, being only double in pitch It is called Dwiguna (double), Dun or Up of the lower note in Indian music and octave in European music

The word octave also denotes the whole range of notes from a particular note to its octave In Indian music this is called a Saptaka [from the seven intervals between the main notes to be mentioned lower down] From the minimum and maximum number of vibrations in musical sounds *viz* 16 and 8192 it will be seen that the whole range of musical sounds is 9 octaves, *viz* 16 vibrations to 32, 32 to 64, 64 to 128, 128 to 256, 256 to 512 512 to 1024, 1024 to 2048, 2048 to 4096 and 4096 to 8192 The human voice extends only to a little over three octaves, from somewhere in the fourth of the above octaves to the seventh So the Indian Music, which was meant specially to deal with singing,—playing on instruments being only a subordinate adjunct,—usually recognises only three octaves or Saptakas These are known as Mandra Stháná Madhya Sthána, and Tára Sthána corresponding to the terms Bass Middle, and Treble in European music, although not having exactly the same relative value as regards pitch. The notes in the Madhya (meaning middle) Sthána are in the easy natural voice emanating from the throat; the Mandra (low tone) Sthána notes require a little exertion of the chest or bosom, and the Tára (high or shrill) notes cause some exertion to the head or brain Hence Shárngdeva in his book *Sangíta Ratnákara* says. "In practice of these three, Mandra is expressed in the chest, Madhya in the throat, and Tára in the head, and they are successively double of the previous one"

The fact that the octave or double of a note is similar to the note itself made the task of fixing other notes relative to a fixed note somewhat easier, for when once the necessary or possible notes required for music were fixed for one of the Saptakas, say Madhyasthána, the notes in the preceding or following Saptakas were to be their halves or doubles respectively.

Chapter III

MUSICAL NOTES

Musical Notes in Harmonic Series, Old Names of the Notes, Vibrations, Interval, *Shrutis*

WHEN a string or wire stretched over two supports is struck, it emits a certain sound. At the same time, the vibration waves striking the two supports and reflecting from them form nodes, dividing the string into numerous sections emitting different sounds, all concordant with the original sound of the whole string. These subsidiary sounds are called harmonics (the original note being known as the fundamental) because the nodes divide the string in the harmonic series of $1, \frac{1}{2}, \frac{1}{3}, \frac{1}{4}, \frac{1}{5}, \frac{1}{6}, \frac{1}{7}, \frac{1}{8}, \frac{1}{9}, \frac{1}{10}$ etc. etc.

Whether the nodes thus generated in strings were observed by the ancients or not is not known. So far is however certain, that the ancient Indians knew that the most concordant notes were produced by the divisions of the string in the above harmonic series. So the Daṇḍa (दण्ड=staff) of their Viná was divided by frets in divisions of $\frac{1}{2}$, $\frac{1}{3}$, $\frac{1}{4}$, $\frac{1}{5}$ (latterly $\frac{1}{6}$ by some) and $\frac{1}{9}$ from the upper support, giving the sounding length of the wire between the frets and the lower support, as $\frac{1}{2}$, $\frac{2}{3}$, $\frac{3}{4}$, $\frac{4}{5}$ and $\frac{8}{9}$, or reversing the order to get the lengths for a rising series of notes as 1, $\frac{8}{9}$, $\frac{4}{5}$, $\frac{3}{4}$, $\frac{2}{3}$, $\frac{1}{2}$. The interval between $\frac{2}{3}$ and $\frac{1}{2}$ being rather big, two notes having $\frac{2}{3}$ the lengths of $\frac{8}{9}$ and $\frac{4}{5}$ respectively, *viz.*, $\frac{16}{27}$ and $\frac{8}{15}$ were introduced, making the set of notes in an octave as 1, $\frac{8}{9}$, $\frac{4}{5}$, $\frac{3}{4}$, $\frac{2}{3}$, $\frac{16}{27}$, $\frac{8}{15}$, $\frac{1}{2}$. The relative vibrations of these notes, which are inversely proportional to the length are—taking the original note as having 480 vibrations—480, 540, 600, 640, 720, 810, 900, 960 The last note being double of the first one forms the first note of the next higher Saptaka

The names given to the above notes in the old days, when chanting of Sámaveda Riks was perhaps the only singing, were as follows:—The original note was known as Krishta (meaning pulled or dragged) perhaps because other notes were derived from it. The next four, which were the harmonics, were known as Prathama (first), Dwitíya (second), Tritíya (third), and Chaturtha (fourth), respectively. The two newly-introduced notes were called Mandra (low tone) and Atiswarya (having a sharp tone) respectively, the one being lower than the other It appears the name Mandra, being a misnomer as compared with the preceding notes, was later changed to Panchama (fifth)

The relation of a note to another is expressed by the ratio of their vibrations This ratio is technically called the "interval" between the two notes Thus the intervals between the eight notes (including the octave), in the ascending order, are 540/480, 600/540, 640/600, 720/640, 810/720, 900/810, and 960/900, or 9/8, 10/9, 16/15, 9/8, 9/8, 10/9, and 16/15

The relative number of vibrations in the sixth note is taken in European music to be 800 instead of 810, so the fifth and sixth intervals are 10/9 and 9/8, respectively, instead of 9/8 and 10/9 in the Indian music

In European music the ratio 9/8 is called a major tone, 10/9 a minor tone, and 16/15 a major semitone Other ratios are known as major or minor seconds, thirds, fourths, etc, and are defined by combinations of these tones or semitones

In the language of Indian Music these ratio fractions are expressible by the number of Shrutis between the two notes, thus avoiding the cumbrous calculations. Shrutis (from Sanskrit श्रु shru, to hear) are fixed notes with the smallest possible intervals compatible with each of them being heard as distinct from its adjacent notes. Besides expressing the intervals between the main notes of the octave, for which they were specially designed, they also help in finding out positions of concordant intermediate notes, as being at certain fixed intervals, they are themselves in consonance with the main notes.

The fraction 9/8 being approximately equal to $(16/15)^2$ and 10/9 equal to $(16/15)^{\frac{3}{2}}$ these interval fractions are approximately in the proportion of 4, 3, and 2. Hence the interval ratio 9/8 is represented by 4 shrutis, the ratio 10/9 by 3 shrutis, and 16/15 by 2 shrutis. Therefore the whole interval between the first note Krishta and its octave is $4 + 3 + 2 + 4 + 4 + 3 + 2$ or 22 shrutis. Let us see if by mathematical calculation the numbers of shrutis as taken and making up the total 22, correspond with the intervals.

Let the notes Krishta etc be denoted by K, I, II, III, IV, V, A, and K^1. We know that if the interval between two notes be divided into a certain number of parts, the number of parts between the first note and any intermediate note varies as the logarithm of the interval, so that if n be the number of parts and i the interval, n varies as $\log i$ or $n = c \log i$ (c being a constant)

Taking the case K and K^1 – $n=22$, $i=2$

$$c = n/\log i = 22/\log 2 = 22/.30103 = 73.08$$

For K and I, $n = c \log i = 73.08 \log 540/480 =$ 3 74, say 4

For K and II $n=73$ 08 log 600/480=7 08, say 7

For K and III, $n=73$ 08 log 640/480=9 13, say 9

For K and IV, $n=73$ 08 log 720/480=12 87, say 13

For K and V, $n=73$ 08 log 810/480=16 61, say 17

For K and A, $n=73$ 08 log 900/480=19 95, say 20

For K and K^1, $n=22$ as taken

So the number of shrutis, for the intervals between the notes, works out to 4, 3, 2, 4, 4, 3, 2, as taken by the Indian musicians. This explains why the number of shrutis was taken as 22, and shows that it was based on scientific principles. Any other number than 22 could, no doubt, have been taken, but then the convenient number like 4, 3, 2, could not have been obtained for the intervals, unless the number was a multiple of 22. As a matter of fact, some musicians of old took 66 shrutis. Kohala writes,

"द्वाविंशतिं केचिदुदाहरन्ति श्रुतीः श्रुति ज्ञान विचार दक्षाः ।
षट् षष्टि भिन्नाः खलु केचिदासामानन्त्यमेव प्रतिपादयन्ति ॥"

i. e., some experts in the knowledge of shrutis take 22 shrutis, others take 66, and some expound that they can be innumerable.

The import of the shrutis and their utility have, it seems, long been forgotten, as the writings of many of the present-day authors of works on music show an ignorance of the subject. Chatura Pandita, the author of the Sanskrita work "Laksha Sangítam," sees it fit to question, the use of Shrutís and asks for the rules about them Some authors make the number 22 as corresponding to the 22 Nádís in the body. Others try to show that there could be more than 22 shrutis or distinct audible sounds in an octave Shárngdeva, the author of "Ratnákara," has been held in ridicule for making a Viná with 22 strings corresponding to the sounds of the 22 shrutis There seems to be no justification for all this

Sangíta Darpana gives the following characteristics of shrutis —नैत्य गीतोपयोगित्वमभिज्ञेयत्वसुगम i e, they are fixed (in relation to each other), useful for the purposes of singing, distinguishable (from the adjacent ones), and in good concordant relations with other notes They were allotted beautiful names, which, as given in Nárada's Sangíta Makaranda, were as follows Prasuná (प्रसूना), Siddhá (सिद्धा), Prabhávatí (प्रभावती), Kántá (कान्ता) Suprabhá (सुप्रभा), Shikhá (शिखा), Diptimati (दीप्तिमती), Ugrá (उग्रा), Hládi (ह्लादी), Nirviri (निर्वीरी), Dirá (दिरा), Sarpasahá (सर्पसहा), Kshánti (क्षान्ति), Vibhúti (विभूति), Máliní (मालिनी), Chapalá (चपला), Bálá (बाला), Sarvaratná (सर्वरत्ना), Shántí (शान्ता), Vikal ní (विकलिनी), Hridayonmaliní (हृदयोन्मलिनी), and Visarini (विसारिणी) The note Krishta was on Prasúná

These names were later on replaced and the following substituted for which are also given the number of vibrations, on the name datum as taken above for the main notes.

0.	Kshobhiní (क्षोभिणी)	490	vibrations.
1.	Tívrá (तीव्रा)	486	"
2.	Kumudvatí (कुमुद्वती)	506 512	"
3.	Mandá (मन्दा)	533	"
4.	Chhandovatí (छान्दोवती)	540	"
5.	Dayávatí (दयावती)	562 569	"
6.	Ranjaní (रंजनी)	576	"
7.	Raktiká (रक्तिका)	600	"
8.	Raudrí (रौद्री)	607 612	"
9.	Krodhí (क्रोधी)	640	"
10.	Vajriká (वज्रिका)	648	"
11.	Prasariní (प्रसारिणी)	675 683	"
12.	Prítí (प्रीतिः)	711	"
13.	Márjaní (मार्जनी)	720	"
14.	Kshiti (क्षितिः)	729	"
15.	Raktá (रक्ता)	759 767	"
16.	Sandípiní (संदीपिनी)	800	"

17	Alápini (आलापिनी)	810	vibrations
18	Madantí (मदन्ती)	844	„
19	Rohini (रोहिणी)	864	„
20	Ramyá (रम्या)	900	„
21	Ugrá (उग्रा)	911 918	„
22	Kshobhini in octave (क्षोभिणी)	960	„

It will be seen that the number of vibrations of Kshobhiní is the same as that of the starting note Krishta, of Chhandovatí the same as that of Prathama Raktiká has the same as Dvitíya, Krodhí the same as Tritíya, Marjaní the same as Chaturtha Alápiní the same as Panchama, and Ramyá the same as Atisvarya The intermediate ones have been calculated by the ratios representing 4, 3, or 2, shrutis from one or other of the main notes In some cases, two values have thus come in

From the number of vibrations for the main notes and the shrutis, it will be noticed that a full Saptaka (of eight notes) could be divided into two equal parts each with four notes, (*e g* Krishta to Tritíya and Chaturtha to higher Krishta, or

Prathama to Chaturtha and Panchama to higher Prathama) the number of vibrations in the second set being respectively one and a half times those in the first set. The first set is called Púrvánga (first part) and the second set is called Uttaránga (latter part) of the Saptaka The octave of the European music does not divide itself exactly in this way

---

Chapter IV

MUSICAL NOTES—(*continued*)

New names how fixed, Standardising of Notes, Grama Changes effected, Present day Main Notes

IN the previous chapter we have seen how the seven main notes and their intermediate notes known as Shrutis were fixed They served all right so far as the singing of songs or poetry was concerned But scientific treatment of the subject necessitated that music should be separated from poetry, which in turn required that it should have its own language This meant that each note should be expressible by a single letter or syllable so that when combined together to form a tune they might be quickly and easily pronounced The selection fell on the letters स् र्, म्, प्, न्, ध् and ग् of the alphabet, to be used in the monosyllabic forms of स (sa) रि (ri), म (ma) प (pa), नि (ni) ध (dha) and ग (ga) The selection was perhaps the best that could be made for easy and quick pronunciation, the gutturals (excepting ग), the palatals and linguals, as also hard letters (except प), and aspirates (except ध), having been avoided.

It was next necessary to find words, beginning with these letters for the names of the notes. Krishta from which the notes started was given the name Nisháda (meaning 'seated'); Prathama was named Swara (the note), because it was the first or the chief note Panchama retained its name. Chaturtha was called Madhyama (middle) as being the midway note between the chief note Prathama and its octave. To accommodate the rest of the letters (रि, ग, and ध), Dwitíya, Tritíya, and Atiswarya, were named Rishabha, Gándhára, and Dhaivata respectively, owing, it appears, to their position on the Shrutís named Ugrá, Nirvírí, and Haridayonmaliní (older names). The word 'Ugra' meaning 'powerful' and 'formidable' and also being an epithet of God Shiva, suggested 'Rishabha' meaning 'a bull.' Nirvíra, meaning a woman whose husband and children are dead suggested Gándhára, Gándhári being the mother of the hundred Kauravas killed in the great war of Mahábhárata. The word Dhaivata seems to have been derived somehow from Dhava (धव),

meaning a rogue or a cheat, Hridayonmalina (black hearted) meaning the same The chief note swara was also named Shadja (षड्ज, meaning born of six), the derivation of which has not been satisfactorily established One of the explanations defines Shadja as that which is produced by the application together of the nose, throat, bosom, palate, tongue, and teeth These parts of the body are not exclusively used in sounding the Shadja note, so the explanation is hardly satisfactory The beautiful names of the notes coined over 2000 years ago are still in use

To recapitulate, the notes of the Indian music with their relative number of vibrations and intervals are noted below :—

Old names.	Later names	Monosyllabic names	Number of vibrations	Intervals
Krishta	Nishada	नि	480	$\frac{9}{8}$ or 4 shrutis.
Prathama	Swara or Shadja	स	540	$\frac{10}{9}$ or 3 shrutis.
Dwitíya	Rishabha	रि	600	$\frac{16}{15}$ or 2 shrutis.
Tritiya	Gándhára	ग	640	$\frac{9}{8}$ or 4 shrutis.
Chaturtha	Madhyama	म	720	$\frac{9}{8}$ or 4 shrutis.
Panchama	Panchama	प	810	$\frac{10}{9}$ or 3 shrutis.
Atiswarya	Dhaivata	ध	900	$\frac{16}{15}$ or 2 shrutis.
Krishta	Nishâda	नि	960	$\frac{9}{8}$ or 4 shrutis.
Prathama	Swara	स	1080	

The number of vibrations representing the pitch of the notes are, as explained so far, relative to each other, bearing the ratios known as the intervals But, with the improvement of science in the present day, instruments have been devised which can with great accuracy measure the number of vibrations in any note or sound, so that particular notes can be standardized This has been done, and the treble *c* (स in the Tarasthána) is taken to be the note having 540 vibrations, the number varies slightly in different countries The other notes have vibrations relatively to this according to their intervals The old Indian music makers also, it appears, thought of standardizing the main notes, but it was not possible at the time They fixed up animals, generally screaming in the same pitch, whose voices in their opnion corresponded with the notes in pitch, not necessarily in the same octave They say

षड्ज मयूरो वदति गवास्तु ऋषभ भाषिणा
अजादि यान्तु गांधार क्रौंच क्वणति मध्यम
पुष्प साधारणे काले पिक कुजति पचमम्
धैवत हेषते वाजि निषाद बृ हिते गज

i e, the peacock cries Shadja, the cow lows in Rishabha, the goats bleat in Gandhara, the heron sounds Madhyama. In spring-time, the Indian cuckoo cries out Panchama, the horse neighs in Dhaivata, and the elephant screams in Nishâda. Sangítá Ratnákara gives the bird Chátaká as uttering Rishabha, and a frog Dhaivata, instead of a cow and horse respectively This is at best a very crude method of fixing the sounds of the notes Nobody has ever tried to see whether the voices of these animals have the same number of vibrations as the notes they represent have. The voices themselves do not continue in the same pitch.

The above table has been continued up to the higher Shadja (स), as स being the chief note the octave is generally taken from स to स. The octave may be taken from any note to its double. In Egyptian music, the octave was perhaps taken from ग to ग; in Grecian music (Dorian) from रि to रि. In order however that the notes be concordant, it was considered necessary that the series of the intervals as noted, *viz.*, 4, 3, 2, 4, 4, 3, 2 shrutis of the Indian music, or 4, 3, 2, 4, 3, 4, 2 shrutis of the European music, or similar scales should be kept up The series of notes with these intervals was known as the Diatonic scale in the European music and Gràma (ग्राम) in the Indian

The term Gráma is now less understood even than the shrutis There are very few persons who know what is meant by Gráma and this must be the case, because, when the real importance of the shrutis is forgotten, a Gráma which is a particular arrangement of the shrutis cannot surely be understood The old Indian music before the time of Bharata (author of *Natya Shastra*, Circa, 4th Century A D) recognised three Grámas, Shadja gráma Madhyama grama, and Gándhára gráma Shadja gráma is the scale noted above (*vide* Table), the other two Grámas are obtained by having the interval shrutis counted from Madhyama and Gándhára respectively in place of Shadja The three Grámas are shown below, side by side with reference to shrutis —

Serial No of Shrutis	Shadja Grama	Madhyama Gráma	Gandhara Grama
0 or 22	Nishada	Nishada	Nishada
1	—	—	—
2	—	—	—
3	—	—	Shadja
4	Shadja	Shadja	—

Serial No of Shrutis	Shadja Gráma	Madhyama Gráma	Gandhara Gráma.
5	—	—	Rishabha.
6	—	—	—
7	Rishabha	Rishabha	—
8	—	—	—
9	Gandhara	Gandhara	Gandhara
10	—	—	—
11	—	—	—
12	—	—	Madhyama.
13	Madhyama	Madhyama	—
14	—	—	Panchama.
15	—	—	—
16	—	Panchama	—
17	Panchama	—	—
18	—	Dhaivata	Dhaivata
19	—	—	—
20	Dhaivata	—	—
21	—	—	—
22	Nishada	Nishada	Nishada.

It will be seen that Madhyane Gráma differs from Shadja Gráma only in the position of प which is one shruti lower, and of ध which is two shrutis lower than in the latter In actual use in Madhyama Gráma, ध was used at the 20th Shruti as in Shadja Gráma, and was four shrutis from Madyama Grama प, but Shárngdeva still took it as a Vikrita Swara for Madhyama Grama Gandhara Grama however differs very considerably, as excepting नि (and of course ग) every note is different, स and म being one shruti lower, रि and ध two shrutis and प three shrutis lower This gráma was therefore very inconvenient to sing and was given up by the time Bharata wrote his *Natyashastra* At the time of Shárngdeva (the author of *Sangita Ratnakar*, 12th century A D) therefore only the first two gramas were in use Later on, Madhyama Gráma was also merged into Shadja Gráma, which is the only grama now in use About the Grama, Chaturdandiprakásha says —' Of these gramas, the Gandhára Gráma is not on the surface of the earth It is agreed by all that it is used in Swargaloka (Heaven) With us, even Madhyana gráma is not existing, in Madhyama gráma Panchama has only three shrutis *Sangita*

Sárámrita has the following on the same subject :—" In the Shástra written by Bharata there are two grámas, Shadja and Mahyama. In Shadja gráma, Panchama has its position at the 17th shruti, but in this (Madhyama Gráma) it stands at the sixteenth shruti. In the current (लक्ष्य) music, Madhyama Gráma is not to be seen. All the musicians sing songs dependent only on Shadja gráma which is the chief gráma now.'

As time went on, the real gráma ratios were also not adhered to, probably because they were forgotten. The notes were fixed by measurement on the danda (दण्ड=staff) of the Víná. They did not however differ much from the older notes. *Sangíta Pârijáta* (by Ahobala Pandita) determines its notes is following manner : "The Tárasthána Shadja is found at the middle point of the Víná danda ; at the middle of the two Shadjas, is Madhyama ; dividing the Víná in three parts we get Panchama ; at the middle point of Shadja and Panchama stands Gándhara ; in the first half of the distance between स and प Rishabha is to be fixed ; at the middle of प and स (double) comes Dhaivata ; and leaving two parts of the distance (between प and स double) is the position of Nisháda."

This gives the number of vibrations to the different notes taking those of स as 540, as ग 648, म 720, प 810, ध 92ა $\frac{5}{7}$, नि 9‾2 and स (double) —1080 रि has not been definitely fixed It will be seen (*Cf* table on page 30) that Gándhára, Dhaivata, and Nishádá differ from our gráma notes, the first and third by one shruti, the second by rather more

The European music follows the gráma, except for the slight difference in two intervals (five and six) as noted already One chief difference however is that the first interval of 9/8 (or *four shrutis*) is taken between स and नि instead of between नि and स of the old Indian music, and the other intervals follow accordingly The numbers of vibrations therefore are स 540, रि 607$\frac{1}{2}$, ग 675, म 720, प 810, ध 900, नि 1022$\frac{1}{2}$ and स (double) 1080 Comparing with the notes in the table given on p 30 the notes रि, ग and नि, are sharper in the European music The English letters indicating the seven notes commencing from स are C, D, E, F, G, A, and B

The Indian music of the present day has the same notes as the European music with alteration in the fifth and sixth intervals as in the old Indian music, so that the vibrations for (ध) *come to* 911$\frac{1}{4}$

instead of 900. Why and when the change from the old notes took place is not known. To connect the new notes with shrutís it has been said that Shadja of the present day has been fixed at the first shrutí (Tívrá) instead of the fourth [Chhandovatí]. This explanation is neither satisfactory nor correct. The change must have taken place very recently, for none of the old Sanskrita books on music recognise this. The change however makes little difference, as all these notes are included among the old notes, either as main or the intermediate ones, so the only effect of the change is that some of the old main notes are now taken as intermediate notes, and *vicé versa*. This will be dealt with in the next chapter. We may conclude this chapter after noting the intervals taken by Pythagoras, the Grecian philosopher, who first attempted the numerical evaluation of musical intervals of European music. His intervals were 9/8, 9/8, 256/243, 9/8, 9/8, 9/8, and 256/243, the first being between Do (स) and Re (रि). His number of vibrations, taking those for स as 540, would thus work out to स (540), रि ($607\frac{1}{2}$), ग ($683\frac{7}{16}$); 7/16, म(720), प(810), ध ($811\frac{1}{4}$), नि ($1025\frac{5}{32}$) and स double (1080).

Chapter V

VIKRITA NOTES

Vikrita Notes based on Shrutis Comparison of the Notes used at different times Reduction of the number a disadvantage

WE have, in the previous chapters, discussed how the main notes of the Indian music, both old and new, were fixed These are known as Shuddha Swaras (शुद्ध स्वर) or pure notes We have however seen that some of the old Shuddha Swarás (रि, ग, ध, and नि) are no more considered as Shuddha in the present day Hindustání music in which these notes with a little higher pitch are taken as Shuddha This is not the case in the music in the South, which almost follows the old notes

The notes which are not Shuddha are called Vikrita (विकृत), meaning "Modified" but they have to be in concordant relations with some of the main notes They are thus defined in Chatura Pandita's *Lakshya Sangita*, quoting from *Sangíta Sarámrita*

स्वरस्तु प्रच्युतः श्रुत्या नियताया यदा भवेत् ।
तदा तस्य विकृतत्वमंगी कुर्वन्ति पण्डिताः ॥

i. e., when a note falls from its position in such a way as to be controlled by shrutis its Vikritatwa (modification) is accepted by the Panditas.

We have dealt with three Shruti intervals, *viz.*, 9/8 or four shrutis, 10/9 or three shrutis, and 16/15 or two shrutis. These are otherwise named respectively as Kákalí (काकलि), meaning "sweet"; Sádhárana (साधारण) or "ordinary"; and antara (अन्तर) or "intermediate". Mention has been made in some of the comparatively recent Sanskrita books of five shrutis and six shrutis intervals also. This will be noted lower down.

Shárngdeva mentions twelve Vikrita notes found according to shruti intervals, in the following manner, thus forming with the seven Shuddha notes, nineteen notes altogether :

Shuddha Shadja being four shrutis from Nishâda, he takes another Shadja (called च्युत or fallen Shadja) at three shrutis. Then he takes one Vikrita Shadja at two shrutis interval from each of these two (*i. e.*, च्युत and शुद्ध) shadjas.

Vikrita Rishbha has been taken at four shrutis interval from Shuddha Shadja

Gándhára being two shrutis from Rishabha, its Vikritas are taken one at three shrutis from Rishabha, and the other at two shrutis from itself These are known as Sádhárana Gandhára and Antara Gándhára respectively

Madhyama has, like Shadja, two Vikrita forms being at four shrutis intervals from Sádhárana and Antara Gándháras respectively

Panchama becomes Vikrita in Madhyama gráma by having four shrutis interval, this gráma having only a three shrutis interval between Madhyama and Panchama

Dhaivata, which is at two shrutis interval from Panchama in Madhyama gráma gets Vikrita at four shrutis in that grama

Nishada, which is at a two shrutis interval from Dhaivata becomes Vikrita at three and four shrutis, and is known as Kaishika nishada and Kákali nishada respectively The word "Kaishika" means "fine", and is applied to a note one shruti higher than the main note, in the same way as "chyuta" denotes a note one shruti lower

These Vikrita notes were not all considered necessary by later musicians, who rejected or added notes according to the requirements of music in their times.

Rágavibodha by Somanáth Pandita, which has the same Shuddha swaras as Ratnákara, considers only seven Vikrita swaras necessary, *viz.*, Chyuta Shadja (called Mridu Shadja), the two Gándháras, and the two Nishádas of Ratanákara, together with a Mridu Madhyama and a Mridu Panchama being at three Shrutis from Shuddha Gándhára and Shuddha Madhyama respectively.

Swaramela Kalánidhí has also the same fourteen notes (seven Shuddha and seven Vikrita) as Rágavibodha. The names of some of the notes have however been altered according to the usage of the notes at the time. Chyuta Shadja being allied to Nishúda was called Chyuta Shadja Nishúda, Mridu Madhyama was called Chyuta Madhyama Gándhara, Mridu Panchama was named Chyuta Panchama Madhyama. In the case of Antara Gándhara being treated as Shuddha, the Shuddha Gándhára was called Panchashruti Rishabha, and Sádhárana Gándhára Shatshruti Rishbha. Similarly, according to the position of

Nishada, the Shuddha and Kaishika Nishadas were known as Panchashruti and Shatshruti Dhaivatas respectively

This introduces us to two new intervals of five shrutis and six shrutis, and at the same time suggests that Gándhára and Nisháda may be taken as Shuddha at a higher pitch The new intervals work out to be —five shrutis$=10/9 \times 16/15=32/27$, and six shrutis$=9/8 \times 16/15=6/5$ A six shruti interval may also be $10/9 \times 10/9 = 100/81$ These are in fact ratios between some of the notes and their thirds, as between स and ग, रि and म, etc

Chaturadandi prakáshika and Sangíta Saramrita recognise only five Vikrita notes, making up, with the seven main notes twelve notes altogether These are the two Gandharas and the two Nishadas of Ratnakara, and also its Vikrita Madhyama named in these works as Varali Madhyama Here Shadja and Panchama are taken as Achala Swaras [unchangeable notes] Also Rishabha and Dhaivata have no Vikritas

Sangíta Parijáta has a peculiar way of reckoning its notes It takes Shadja and Panchama as Achala, and each of the remaining five notes as-having six degrees of pitch differing by one Shruti. In an ascending scale, the six degrees are named Púrva (first), Komala (soft), Shuddha (pure), Tívra (sharp), Tívratara (sharper), and Tivratama (sharpest) The gamut or Saptaka is divided into twenty-two parts or shrutis, and the Shuddha swaras are fixed as in Ratnákara, Komala and Púrva then precede, and Tivra, Tívratara, and Tívratama, follow the Shuddha note. Many of the notes overlap in this way and consequently have two names. The author, Ahobala Pandita, then says that ten notes of these, *viz*, Púrva and Tívra Rishabha, Tívratara and Tívratama Gándhára, Tivra and Tívratama Madhyama, Púrva and Tívra Dhaivata, and Tívratara and Tívratama Madhyama, Púrva and Tívra Dhaivata, and Tívratara and Tívratama Nishada have to be left out in the then current music. This left only twelve notes.

The present-day Indian music also takes notice of only twelve notes, *viz*, seven Shuddha and five Vikritas. As we have seen, however, the Shuddhas of the notes रि, ग, ध, and नि, now are sharper than those in the old Indian music. This is due to the first interval of four shrutis having been taken between स and रि instead of नि and स, so that

Shuddha रि is sharper by one shruti, ग by two shrutis ध by one shruti and नि by two shrutis The Vikritas are komala रि, ग ध and नि, at two shrutis interval from the next lower Shuddha swaras स, रि, प and ध respectively, also Tivra म at a two shrutis interval below प, and sometimes the same interval above Shuddha म

These Vikrita notes introduce to us one more interval, *viz* one shruti interval, *i e*, the one between a Vikrita note and the closer of the two main notes between which the Vikrita occurs When the interval between the main notes is three shrutis, the value of the one shruti interval is 25/24, and when the interval is four shrutis it is 81/80 The former is called a chromatic semitone in European music, and is the interval by which the notes are generally sharpened and flattened in wha is called the chromatic scale The one shruti interval in the Pythagorean scale, we have seen, is $\frac{256}{243}$

The names of all the notes, according to the different works on music, are given below, side by side, for the sake of comparison —

Shrutis	Notes taken from Ratnakara	Notes taken from Ragavibodha	Notes taken from Swaramela Kalanidhi.	Notes taken from Chaturadandi Prakashika and Sangita Saramrita	Notes taken from Sangita Parijata.	Notes taken from current Indian music.
1						
2						
3	Chyuta Shadja.	Mridu Shadja.	Chyuta Shadja Nishada	—	—	—
4	Shuddha Shadja.	Shuddha Shadja	Shuddha Shadja.	Shuddha Shadja	Shuddha Shadja	Shuddha Shadja.
5	Kaishika Shadja.	—	—	—	—	—
6	Antara Shadja	—	—	—	Komala Rishabha	Komala Rishabha.
7	Shuddha Rishabha,	Shuddha Rishabha	Shuddha Rishabha.	Shuddha Rishabha.	Shuddha Rishabha or Purva Gandhavra.	—

8	Vikrita Rishabha	—	—	—	—	Shuddha Rishabha
9	Shuddha Gandhara	Shuddha Gandhara	Shudda Gandhara or Pancha Shruti Rishabha	Shuddha Gandhara	Shuddha Gandhara or Tivratara Rishabha	—
10	Sadharana Gandhara	Sadharana Gandhara.	Sadharana Gandhara or Shat shruti Ri shabha	Sadharana Gandhara	Tivratama Rishabha or Tivra Gandhara	Komala Gandhara
11	Antara Gan dhara	Antara Gan dhara	Antara Gan dhara	Antara Gan dhara	—	Shuddha Gandhara
12	—	Mridu Madh yama	Chyuta Ma dhyam Gandhara	—	—	—
13	Shuddha Ma dhayama	Shuddha Ma dhayama	Shuddha Madhyma	Shuddha Madhyama	Shuddha Madhya	Shuddha Madhyama

Shrutis	Notes taken from Ratankara	Notes taken from Ragavibodha.	Notes taken from Swaramela Kalanidhi	Notes taken from Chaturadandi Prakashika and Sangita Saramrita	Notes taken from Sangita Parijata.	Notes taken from current Indian music.
14	Kaishika Madhyama	—	—	—	—	—
15	Vikrita Madhyama.	—	—	Varali Madhyama	Tivratara Madhyam.	Tivra Madhyama.
16	Madhyama Grama Panchama.	Mridu Panchama.	Chyuta Panchama Madhayama		—	—
17	Shuddha Panchama or Vikrita M g Panchama.	Shuddha Panchama.	Shuddha Panchama	Shuddha Panchama.	Shuddha Panchama	Shuddha Panchama
18	Madhyama grama Dhaivata	—	—	—	—	—

19	—	—	—	—	Komala Dhaivata	Komala Dhaivata
20	Shuddha Dhaivata or Vikrita m g Dhaiva ta	Shuddha Dhaivata	Shuddha Dhaivata,	Shuddha Dhaivata	Shuddha Dhaivata or Purva Nishada	—
21	—	—	—	—	—	Shuddha Dhaivata
22	Shuddha Nishada	Shuddha Nishada	Shuddha Nishada or Panch ashruti Dhaivata	Shuddha Nishada	Shuddha Nishada or Tiva ratara Dhaivata	—
1	Kaishika Nishada	Kaishika Nishada	Kaishika Nishada or Shatshru ti Dhaivata	Kaishika Nishada	Tivratama Dhaivata or Tivra Nishada	Komal Nishada
2	Kakali Ni shada	Kakali Ni shada	Kakali Ni shada	Kakali Ni shada	—	Shuddha Ni shada
3						
4						

Going through the comparative table given above, two facts are noticeable:

(1) The number of notes has gradually decreased; while it was nineteen at the time Ratnákara was written, it is only twelve at the present day.

(2) There is a tendency of equalising the intervals between the notes.

It is doubtful if the reduction in the number of notes has been to any advantage. The higher Indian music, which follows nature generally, requires in most cases that, in going from one note to another, the approach should be gradual, as is noticed in Rágálpana. It is only the light music which approaches its notes in leaps as it were. The reduced number of notes, *viz.*, twelve, is quite enough for the latter, but hardly for the former. It is true an accomplished singer will not care whether the notes which he utters are in the gamut or not, and will go through all the necessary gradations of sound, but a beginner has to go by the notes he learns, and so his production is likely to sound like a series of distinct notes rather than a well-blended piece. We notice a gradual replacement of higher music and álápana by lighter music, and a growing love for theatrical songs This must, to a certain extent at least, be attributed to the gradual disappearance of the old Vikrita notes Even European music has more than twelve notes It is a matter for consideration by the experts whether a few intermediate notes should not be re introduced in appropriate places [*see* also Chap VII]

The equalisation of intervals is a natural consequence of the reduction of the number of the Vikrita notes The intervals, in order that there be concordance, have however to be those already noticed This comes in the way of exact equalisation But in the case of instruments with a key board similar to the piano forte, which can have only a definite number of notes, it is difficult practically to maintain the correct intervals for all the notes, and equalisation has been effected Harmoniums are also constructed on this basis *i e*, the whole interval between a note and its octave is divided into twelve equal intervals of about 106/100 This is known as equal temperament of the notes The music obtained from these instruments is never agreeably in tune; it is deficient in richness of effect and is generally insipid. So, while harmoniums are quite good for beginners to learn music in its elementary stage, their use should be discarded for advanced stages, as their notes are not in the natural concordant relation to each other. The tempered notes are called enharmonic notes.

Chapter VI

SCALES

Grama and Grama Ragas Murchhana, Vikrita notes obtained from Murchhanas, Old Parent *scales*, *Marga and Deshi ragas*

IN the previous chapters we have seen what musical notes were in use at different periods from the time of Ratnakara up to the present day These were not fixed in a haphazard manner, but scientifically After determining the concordant series of intervals in the octave of 22 shrutis taken from स to स, the first attempts were naturally directed towards forming other scales, by putting the different notes successively in place of the main note स, and the subsequent notes following at the correct intervals This gave the different grámas, of which we have seen three were recognised in the old days, the Shadja, the Madhyama and the Gándhára gramas [*vide* table on page 33—34] Of the other four gramas, Nisháda gráma worked out to almost the same as Gándhára gráma Rishabha and Dhaivata grámas, which were similar (except for the position of म), altered the position of Nisháda, from which all the main scales were supposed to start and were hence not adopted as grámas. Panchama was nearly the same as Shadja gráma.

Fixing the three gramas, the next series of scales were formed by placing their main notes स, म, and ग, successively in the position of each of the other notes. Thus for each gráma there were formed seven scales or twenty-one in all. This process was called Múrchhaná (मूर्च्छन = swooning) so called because the main note, as if in a trance, placed itself in the position of each other note. Each such scale was given a name. Múrchhanás for the Shadja gráma are given below. From these and the murchhanás of Madhyama gráma all the vikrita notes of Ratnakara, or for the matter of that of the whole Indian music, are obtained. These have been indicated.

Shruti Interval	Murchhana of स	Murchhana of रि	Murchhana of ग	Murchhana of म	Murchhana of प	Murchhana of ध	Murchhana of नि
	स						
3							
	रि	स					
2							
	ग	रि (Vikrita स or 2 sh रि)	स				
4							
	म	ग (Sadha rana ग)	रि (Vikrita रि)	स			
4							
	प	म (Kaishi ka म)	ग (Chyuta म	रि (Vikrita)	स		
3							
	ध	प	म (Vikrita म)	ग (Antara)	रि	स	
2							
	नि	ध (2 sh ध)	प	म	ग	रि (Vikrita स or 2 sh रि)	स
4							
	स						

Shruti Interval	Murchhana of स.	Murchhana of रि.	Murchhana of ग	Murchhana of म.	Murchhana of प	Murchhana of ध.	Murchhana of नि.
	स	नि (Kaishika नि)	ध (4 sh. ध)	प	म	ग (Sadharana ग)	रि (Vikrita रि)
3							
	रि	स	नि (Kakali नि)	ध	प (Madhyana gramaप)	म	ग (Antara ग)
2							
	ग		स	नि	ध (Madhyana gramaध)	प (Tivra म)	म
4							
	म			स	नि	ध (2 sh ध)	प
4							
	प				स	नि (Kaishika नि)	ध (1Shr. ध)
3							
	ध					स	नि (Kakali नि)
2							
	नि						स
4							
	स						

There were perhaps other methods too of forming scales in old days, but they are not known at present Nor is it possible at this distant age to say which of the old scales then known as grama ragas (ग्राम रागा) corresponded with the scales noted above except of course Shadja and Madhyama gramas Sharngdeva names 30 grama rágas classified under five classes, viz

1 Shuddhas or pure—7 in number,

2 Bhinnas or different, perhaps with a modified series of intervals—5 in number,

3 Gauras perhaps coming from Gaura country—3 in number

4 Vesaras or mixed ones—8 in number, and

5 Sadharana or ordinary, used by the public—7 in number

Sharngdwa says they differed from each other in the absence or presence, more or less, of Vakra or turning notes (see Chapter IX) and Gamakas (tanas and alankaras—Chapter X), in the slow or quick succession of notes, and in the use of the different Sthanas (Tara, Madhya and Mandra Chapter II) He knew only fifteen of these having been used to form rágas or songs. Some of the names of these gráma rágas still obtain in the present-day Indian music, *e.g*, Kukubha and Hindola, but it is difficult to say if the tunes really continue the same. The old scales have thus only an academic interest. The following facts are however noticeable :—(1) The múrchhaná of Panchama is the same as Madhyama gráma, (2) except in this múrchhaná, the note Panchama is a fixed one so far as the Shadja gráma is concerned, (3) The múrchhaná of Nisháda is the same as the current main scale or Shadja gráma of the new Indian music.

The books written after Ratnákara have their own scales called melas (मेला:) or Janak melas [scales from which rágas are derived, the word Janaka, meaning "father"]. These differed from the old scales in that while the latter were derived from the particular series of intervals by the process of grámas and múrchhanás, and were the producers of the several vikrita notes, the post-Ratnákara scales were formed from the shuddha and vikrita notes already found out. and hardly followed any fixed series of intervals. In these Janak melas, the following points are supposed to have been observed —(1) That they should contain all the seven notes whether in the shuddha or vikrita forms, and (2) that the notes should be used in the correct order in both ascent and descent, i e, स, रि, ग, म प, ध, नि in ascent and स नि, ध, प, म, ग, रि, in descent

The Indian terms for ascent and descent are Ârohana (आरोहण) or Anuloma (अनुलोम) and Avarohana (अवरोहण) or Viloma (विलोम) respectively

Rágavibodha mentions 23 Janak melas, and Swarámela Kalánidhi 20 Chaturadandiprakásha and Sangítasáramrita calculate the possible number of Janak melas in the following manner

The octave, we have seen (Chapter III) is divisible in two parts called Purvánga and Uttaránga These are taken one from स to म and the other from प to स [double] For this purpose स, म, and प are taken as fixed, only the intermediate notes रि and ग in Purvanga and ध and नि in Uttaranga are taken as changeable From the table on pages 46—48 it will be seen that these works recognise four variations between स and म, and four variations between प and स [double] The middle two of these having two names in each [*vide* column 4 of the table]. By taking combinations, we therefore get six combinations for each of the two groups, or 6 × 6 = 36 scales altogether. But this is taking म as a fixed note, which is not the case, there being another म called Varalí Madhyama. Hence there can be 36 more scales with this Madhyama, or 72 scales altogether. Names have been allotted to each of these 72 scales.

It will be seen from the table referred to that the interval between some of the notes to form these scales would be only one shruti, which is hardly allowable, and the number of the actually usable scales would be much reduced. As a matter of fact, these two works mention only nineteen of these as in use in their time. Venkateshwara, who calculated out these scales, himself says that he did so only in academical interest

These old scales could not be of much use to us now as their Shuddha रि, ग, ध, and नि, do not find a place on our gamut (*vide* table page 46—48) and although the names of many of the old scales coincide with the present-day scales, strictly speaking the two are not the same The latter therefore require a separate treatment, very much on the same lines no doubt This will be done in the next chapter

It may be mentioned of the later post-Ratnakara writers, to their great credit, that they tried to release music from the fetters of the old grama conventions, even if it was quite scientific, and enlarged its scope, so necessary to the development of a fine art No doubt, in India, the general public has never confined itself to the conventional music, and the songs were from very early times divided into two classes, called Marga (मार्ग) and Deshi (देशी), the former strictly following the rules fixed by the old music makers like Bharata and used in worshipping gods and invoking their blessings, the latter being those sung by different people in different parts of the country according to their taste, thus being more popular and pleasing The present tendency, however, of banishing shrutis or grama out of our music altogether is not very wholesome

—

Chapter VII.

NEW SCALES.

Grama Ragas in Current music; New Vikrita notes obtained from Murchhanas; How Shadja and Panchama become Fixed notes; New Parent Scales worked out.

OUR present main scale is, we have seen, the Nisháda múrchhana of the old main scale, and has the following series of intervals between स and स:—Shadja to Rishabha, 4 shrutis; Rishabha to Gandhara, 3 shrutis; Gandhara to Madhyama, 2 shrutis; Madhyama to Panchama, 4 shrutis; Panchama to Dhaivata, 4 shrutis; Dhaivata to Nishada, 3 shrutis; and Nishada to Shadja (double), 2 shrutis. From this scale, the process of múrchhaná as explained in the previous chapter works out the following seven scales:—

Shruti interval	Murchhana of स	Murchhana of रि	Murchhana of ग	Murchhana of म	Murchhana of प	Murchhana of ध	Murchhana of नि
4	स						
3	रि	स					
2	ग	रि	स				
4	म	ग	रि (Komala)	स			
4	प	म	ग (Komala)	रि	स		
3	ध	प	म (Kaishika)	ग (Kaishika)	रि	स	
2	नि	ध	प	म (Tirva)	ग	रि	स
4	स	नि	ध (Komala)	प	म	ग	रि (Komala)

Shruti interval.	Murchhana of स.	Murchhana of रि.	Murchhana of ग.	Murchhana of म.	Murchhana of प.	Murchhana of ध.	Murchhana of नि.
	रि	स	नि (Komala)	ध	प	म	ग (Komala)
3							
	ग		स	नि	ध (Chyuta)	प	स
2							
	म			स	नि (Chyuta Komala)	ध	प (Tivra म)
4							
	प	Old Shadja-grāma, *vide* table, p 33-34			स	नि	ध (Komala)
4							
	ध					स	नि (Komala)
3							
	नि						स
1							
	स					Old Madhyama-grāma, *vide* table, p 33-34.	

The following facts are noticeable in the above Múrchhana table —(1) The múrchhana of Rishabha is the old Shadja grama main scale

(2) The murchhaná of Dhaivata is the old Madhyama grama

(3) The Múrchhanas of Gándhára, Madhyama, and Nisháda, give all the Vikrita notes in use in the present day music There are two additional modifications of ग and म, each a shruti higher than the Shuddha ग and म They are thus the old Chyuta Madhyama Gándhára and Kaishika Madhyama The Múrchhaná of Panchama also gives ध, and Komala नि, each a shruti lower These are the old Shuddha Dhaivata and Nisháda respectively Although we do not recognise these notes (E sharp or Pythagorean E, F sharp, A, and a semitone flatter B of the European music) as separate notes, they give the correct music, and it is a matter for consideration if any of them should not be re introduced We shall come to this later on

(4) The note Panchama does not undergo any variation, except in the Madhyama grama and the Murchhana of Nishada where it becomes identical with Tívra Madhyama

The fact that a murchhaná of the Shádja gráma could also produce the Madhyama gráma, which was also noticed in the case of the old scales, has helped in the amalgamation of the latter gráma with the former. This, in turn, made the note Shadja as a fixture, for there can now be no scales or rágas (songs) without this note. In the time of Shárngdeva, when Madhyama gráma was in use, in which Madhyama and not Shadja was taken as the chief note, there used to be songs without Shadja.

The amalgamation, or rather abolition, of the Madhyama gráma, which had variations of Panchama also, left this note also as one not undergoing any change. Hence, in the present-day music, स and प are both fixed notes, the former being indispensable at the same time

(5) The Múrchhaná of Madhyama associates the tívra madhyama with Panchama, from which it is two shrutis lower, and with other Shuddha swaras The note also occurs in the Múrchhaná of Nishádá, as a modification of Panchama, where it is two Shrutis higher than the Shuddha म, which is itself present, and is associated with the other Vikrita swaras Tivra म, therefore, suits well

with many of the notes, and is almost next to स in importance

Of these Múrchhaná scales the main one (that of स) is known as Bilavala (old names Shankarabharana or Shankarabhúshana), the Murchhaná of Gándhára, with म a shruti lower, is called Bhairavi that of Madhyama, with म a shrúti lower, is called Yamana or Imana Chatura Pandita prefers to call it Kalyání which is also the old name the other four not being in use now Bhairavi and Kalyani, it may be noted, are the Panchama and Dhaivata múrchhanás respectively of Madhyama grama The three scales, Bilávala Bhairavi, and Kalyani, of the present day music are therefore gráma rágas

Before applying the other process of obtaining scales, it is better, in order to facilitate writing, to give short names to each of the notes (including Vikritas) the full system of notation will be dealt with later on We shall call Shadja as स (sa) Komala Rishabha as रा (ra), Shuddha or Tivra Rishabha as री (ri), Komal Gandhara as गा (ga), Shuddha or Tivra Gandhara as गी (gi) Shuddha or Komal Madhyama as म (ma), Tivra Madhyama as मी (mi) Panchama as प (pa), Komala

Dhaivata as धा (dha), Shuddha or tivra Dhaivata as धी (dhi), Komal Nishạ́da as ना (na), and Shuddha or Tívra Nisháda as नी (ni). These notes in Mandrasthána will be denoted with a hyphen (-) below, and those in Tárasthána with a hyphen above them, *e.g.*, Panchama in mandrasthana will be प (pa), and Shadja double on in Tarasthama as स (sā). The series of notes in a scale or tune is called its sargam (सरगम), the word being composed of the first four notes of the Saptaka.

To form the scales, the saptaka is to be considered as consisting of two parts, the púrvánga (स to म or मी) and the Uttaránga (प to स). The párvánga with म can have four variations, *viz*, (1) स, रा, गा, म, (2) स, रा, गी, म, (3) स, री, गा, म, and (4) स, री, गी, म. Similarly with मी, it has also four variations, *viz.*, (5) स, रा, गा, मी, (6) स, रा, गी, मी, (7) स, री, गा, मी, and (8) स, री, गी, मी. The uttaránga can also have four variations, *viz.*, (I) प, धा, ना, स, (II) प, धा, नी, स, (III) प, धी, ना, स, and IV) प, धी, नी, स. Combining the four variations of the purvánga having म nos. (1) to (4) with those of uttaránga nos. I to IV we get

4 × 4 or sixteen scales Of the purvánga with मी the No (7) is considered a bad combination and is never used, the other three can combine with the variations of uttarange without नाॅ (which is not used with मी), *i e*, nos II and IV So there could be 3 × 2, or six more scales The total number of the parent scales or Janaka melas could therefore be twenty two

Of these the following only seem to be in use —

Number	Combination	Names of the scales	Sargam or the arrangement of the notes
1	1 + I	Bhairavi (भैरवी) old name Todi	स रा गा म प धा ना सॅ
2	2 + I	Vasanta Bhairavi (वसंत भैरवी), also called Bakulabharana (बकुलाभरण)	स रा गी म प धा ना सॅ
3	2 + II	Bhairava (भैरव), old name malava Gauda (मालव गौड)	स रा गी म प धा नी सॅ
4	2 + III	Vegavahini (वेगवाहिनी,) old name	स रा गी म प धी ना सॅ

Number.	Combination	Names of the scales.	Sargam or the arrangement of the notes
5	2 + IV	Chhayavatı (छायावता), old name	स रा गी म प भी नी सं
6	3 + I	Asavarı (आसावरी); old name, Nata-Bhairavı (नट भैरवी)	स री गा म प धा ना स
7	3 + III	Kafi (काफ़ी); old name, Srı (श्री) or Haıprıya.	स री गा म पधी ना सं
8	4 + III	Khammách (खम्माच); old name, Kambhojı (कांभोजी)	स री गी म प धी ना सं
9	4 + IV	Bılavala (विलावल); old name Shankarabharana (शंकराभरण).	स री गी म प धी नी सं
10	5 + II	Todı (तोडी); old name, Varalı (वराली).	स रा गा मी प धा नी सं
11	6 + II	Púrvi (पूर्वी); old name, Ramakrıya (रामक्रिया) and Kàmavárdhana (कामवर्धन).	स रा गी मी प धा नी सं

Number	Combination	Names of the scales	Sargam or the arrangement of the notes
12	6 + IV	Màrvá (मारवा), old name Gamakakriya Gamanashrama (गमकक्रिया, गमनश्रम)	स रा गी मी प धो नी सं
18	8 + IV	Kalyani (कल्याणी) or Iman (यमन)	स री गी मी प धी नी सं

Of these 13 again Nos 2, 4, and 5 are very rarely used, and it is only the remaining 10 that are in common use Chatura Pandita and other music masters like P Vishnu Narayana Bhatkhande, P Vishnu Digambara have therefore fixed upon these 10 janaka melas (parent scales) only It may however be mentioned that neither these 10 scales, nor the 13 mentioned above nor the possible 22 scales, nor even the 72 scales of Venkateshwara, mentioned in Chaturdandi prakashika, can singly be made to cover all the tunes or rágas now current, for there are a good number of those which require the use of both the gandháras, madhyamas, or nishádas For instance, the tunes Iman Kalyána . Kedará,

Kámoda etc., belonging to the Janaka mela Kalyáni, the tunes Kálingrá, Rámakalı, Lalit etc., belonging to Bhairava, and the tunes Púrví, Parja etc., belonging to Purvı, require both the Madhyamas each; the tunes Soratha, Desha, Jaijaiwanti, etc., belonging to Khammách, and the tunes Pılu, Barwa, Mıyan ki Malár etc., belonging to Káfi, each require both the nıshádas This could be met by a few alterations or combination of two or more scales. As an example, Kalyáni may be replaced by a scale having both the madhyamas, *e.g.* Iman Kalyana, which tune has both the Madhyamas; Purvi and Bhairva may be combined under the name Kalıngra which, as in use at present, has both the madhyamas. Sımılarly, Kafi and Khammach may be blended into one Jaıjaıvantı which tune, requires both nıshádas and both gándháras, thus combining the two janaka melas with the advantage of the two nıshádas.

This will further reduce the number of Janaka melas, but the change is not likely to be of any great advantage, as the memory will have to be additionally taxed in the case of the tunes with one madhyama or one nishada only; for after all the Janaka melas apparently serve no others purpose than helping in remembering what swaras (notes) each tune has

The musical instruments which require changing of stays or frets to form different scales, called Thaths (ठाठ) in this case, have some use for the Janaka melas Sitárs and similar instruments, like Táús etc, are perhaps the only such instruments, but they do not confine themselves to the above named ten scales Some works on Sitár recognise more and some less number of scales not necessarily corresponding with the above ten Kalyana, Kalingra, and Jaijaivanti are recognised scales or tháths Desha having two nishadas is also recognised The Sitár in fact is designed to have two madhyamas and, in one of the two sthanas (octaves), two nishadas also as it was realised by the inventor of the instrument that there were several tunes with both forms of these notes

—

Chapter VIII.

RELATION OF NOTES WITH EACH OTHER

Affinity of notes; Samvadis Vivadis &c Shruti necessary to determine affinity; Danger in discarding Shrutis

In Chapter II, it was noticed that two notes differing in pitch are relatively more or less concordant and pleasing to the ear, according to the frequency of coincidences of their vibrations in a given time. The number of vibrations in each note of the present-day Indian music as noted in Chapter IV for the main notes, and for the vikrita notes, as calculated by the shruti intervals of those notes, from the main notes, noted in Chapter V are as follows: स—540, रा—576, री—607½, गा—648, गी—675, म—720, मी—759⅜ or 768 accordingly as it is calculated from प or म, प—810, धा—864, धी—911¼, ना—972, नी—1012½ and सं—1080 The following table shows the number of coincidences in a second, which is the measure of concordance or affinity each note bears with another.

TABLE

Notes	स	रा	री	गा	गी	म	मी	प	धा	धी	ना	नी
स	—											
रा	36	—	—									
री	68	—	—									
गा	108	72	41	—								
गी	135	5	68	—	—							
म	180	144	23	72	45	—						
मी	17	192	152	24	85	48	—					
प	270	18	203	16	135	90	51	—				
धा	108	288	14	216	[illegible]7	144	96	54	—			
धी	34	2	304	20	34	11	152	101	—	—		
ना	108	36	122	324	27	36	12	162	108	61	—	
नी	68	5	203	41	338	28	253	203	14	101	—	—

From the table it is evident (1) that मी with all its association with the Komala notes, as was noticed when múrchhanás were worked out, has little or no affinity with गा and ना, and this is perhaps the reason why ना is never used with मी, and the combination सरीगामी has been discarded [*vide* Chapter VII, page 69].

(2) The highest affinity of the notes is with those at intervals of 13 and 9 shrutis, or expressing in terms of main notes with the 5th and 4th notes. The latter are called Samvádís (संवादी), which term will be explained lower down.

(3) In the cases of गी and धी, and म and नी, which have the relations of 4th and 5th with each other, the matter is however different, the affinity for the pairs being very low. This is due to the fact that the shruti intervals of the two pairs are not 13 and 9, but 12 and 10 in one case and 11 and 11 in the other. स and मी have also the relation of 11—11 and there is little affinity between the two notes It seems necessary that for the first pair, the Dhaivata note should be a shruti flatter than धी, *i.e.*, 3 shrutis above Panchma, or the same note as the old shuddha Dhaivata of the Indian music, or the note A of the Euro-

pean music For the second pair, a new Nishada, a shruti lower than नि or 9 shrutis from म is necessary This is the same as our old shuddha Nishada The introduction of these new Vikrita notes was also indicated by the Múrchhanás [*vide* Chapter VII] The sharpening of गी and म as noted there would not then be necessary

The number of vibrations of the new Dhaivata, which we shall call dh (ध) would be 900 and its affinity with other notes would be स 180, गी 225, म 180, प 90, नी 113, and so with the first three it could be used with a much better advantage than धा or धी Similarly, the number of vibrations of the new Nishada, which we may call n (न) would be 960, and its affinity with सा and म and मी would be 192, 240, and 192 respectively, so that as a samvadi of म and when used with सा it would sound much better than the other forms of Nishada and with मी better than ना For this defect, in no raga or tune is Nishada ever used with Madhyama as its samvadi although the two bear 4th and 5th relations

In respect of their relations and use in ragas or tunes, Ratnákara mentions four classi fications of the notes, *viz*, vádí, samvádí, vívádí, and anuvádí. The note which is frequently used in a raga is called Vadi (वादी, meaning a speaker or dictator) because it determines the character of the tune Two notes which have 8 and 12 shrutis between them, *i.e*, which are at 9th and 13th shrutis from each other, are mutually called samvádís संवादी, meaning similar or equal]. The pairs Nishāda Gándhára and Rishabha-Dhaivata are Vivádís (विवादी meaning quarrelling) to other Vadi notes and to each other. Vivadis form a sort of opposition, as being the second samvadis to the samvadis of the Vadi note, they can assert themselves against the Vadi note, and may alter the import of the tune. In particular cases, therefore, they have to be avoided, or sparingly and carefully used The rest of the notes are called Anuvadis (अनुवादी) which help the Vadi and Samvadi notes, as do the servants their masters.

In our present-day music, as also in the later post Ratnákara music, the last two, *viz*., Vivádi and Anuvádi, have no real significance, although the terms have been preserved The notes left out from a tune, or very sparingly used, are called Vivadis in reference to that tune without any reference to the Vadi note, or giving the reason of their being left out Other terms used for a Vadi note are Ansha (अंश, meaning "the chief part") and Jiva (जीव = life) Vivadi notes are known as Varjita (वर्जित=disallowed) Ananyasta or Astapráya (अनन्यास्त, अस्तप्राय=almost thrown out or absent), and Manaksparsha (मनाक्स्पर्श = very little touched) according to their use

The following table gives the Samvádi Vivádi notes etc, as defined in Ratnákara

Vadi	Samvadi	Vivadi	Anuvadi
स	प	रि, ध	ग, म, नि
,,	म	नि, ग	रि, प, ध
र	ध	ग नि	स, म, प
,,	प	—	स, ग, म, ध, नि
ग	नि	—	स, रि, म प, ध
,	ध	रि	स, म, प, नि

Vadi	Samvadı.	Vıvadı.	Anuvadı.
म	स	—	रि, ग, प, ध, नि
,,	नि	ग, ध	स, रि, प
प	रि	ध, ग	स, म, नि
,,	स	—	रि, ग, म, ध, नि
ध	ग	नि	स, रि, म, प
,,	रि	—	स, ग, म, प, नि
नि	म	—	स, रि, ग, प, ध
,,	ग	ध,	स, म, प

It will be seen that the chief vıvádıs are the main notes eıther followıng or preceding the vádı main notes (the other being only the second samvádı of the same). When these positions are occupied by स, म or प, there ıs no vıvádi, as ıt ıs only the नि, ग, रि and ध that become vivadis according to Ratnákara In the present sense of the term, प and म do become vıvadıs. However स being the main note it has always to be assisted by one or the other of its samvádıs म and प,

so that there can now be no tune with both म and प being absent मो may take the place of म in certain cases

The interval between two adjacent notes is, we know, 2, 3, or 4 shrutis, and sometimes according to some books 5 or 6 shrutis also, but the latter are, in fact, ratios between a note and its third, almost invariably in the case of the 6 shrutis interval Hence as vivadis form adjacent notes, we may conclude that intervals of 2, 3, 4, and 5 shrutis do not make for affinity, *i e*, the pairs with intervals 2 20, 3 19, 4 18, and 5 17 are bad combinations The pair 8 14 is also not found a good combination in practice, probably because this interval always occurs between a tivra (sharp) and a komala (flat) note (*e g*, between गी and धा, म and धीं and मो and ना) which combination, excepting the case of मो already noticed, is incongruous Among the fourths and fifths (samvadis) we have already seen 11 11 and 12 10 are not good combinations, although the latter is not infrequently allowed for want of a correct Dhaivata in the present gamut Hence the pairs of notes having good affinity are those with 9 13, 7 15, and 6 16 intervals This is evident from the affinity table also

The following statement gives the notes in a more convenient form showing the comparative affinity of each note, main as well as vikrita, with the rest It divides the latter in four parts : (*a*) are the samvadis, *i e.*, those having 13-9 shruti intervals, (*b*) the anuvadis, with 7-15 and 6-16 shruti intervals, (*c*) the neutrals which I shall call nirvádís and which include vivadis, and (*d*) vivadis separately, which term must, I think, be confined to its original sense given in Ratnakara as interpreted and explained above. These are generally with 4-18 and sometimes 3-19 shruti intervals. Madhyama and Panchana have also been shown here although not taken in Ratnakara.

Statement showing relations of notes to each other.

Notes.	Sam-vadis.	Anuvadis	Nirvadis	Vivadis.
स	प, म	ध, गी, गा, धा	ना, री, रो, रा, धी, मी	री, न
रा	धा, मी	धी, म, न	गा, स, ला, प. गी, नी	गा, नी
रो	धी, प	नी, मी, ना	स, गी, गा, म, धा	गी (nearly)

Notes	Sam vadis	Anuvadis	Nirvadis	Vivadi
गा	ना धा	प, स	रा, म री नी, मो धी	रा
गी	नी, ध	स, प	मी, री, म, धी, धा, ना, रा	मी, री (nearly)
म	न, स	ध, धा, रा	प, गा मो गी, री, ना, नी धो	प
मो	नी, रा	न, री, धो	धा, गी, प म, गा स, ना	गी धा
प	स, री	नी, गा, ना, गी	धी म, धा, मी रा	म, धो
धा	रा	म, स	ना, मी, प, गी री, नो	मी, न ।
धी	री	रा, मी	प, नी, ना स गी, गा म	प
ना	गा	प, री	स, धा, धी, रा म, गी, मी	धा
नी	गी, मी	री, प	धी, स, गा म, धा, रा	ध रा

From the above statement it would be evident how defective it is to take the samvadis as 4th or 5th notes from the Vadi note, without any reference to the interval, but this has to be done after discarding shrutis, which is the present day tendency For instance, taking Panchama as a samvadi of rishabha when the latter is komala will surely be incorrect but yet it is shown as such Chatura Pandita in his *Laksha Sangita* and Md Nawábali Khan in his *Maarifun Nagmat* do so in the case of the tunes Gauri (गौरि) and Shriraga श्रीराग) which are included in the Purvi mela, and have komala rishabha (*i.e.*, रा). The ridiculous portion of the thing is that the latter book while mentioning प as samvádi gives a Lachchhan gíta (a song showing the characteristics of a tune, from लक्षण meaning peculiarities or characteristics) of Gauri which has no प in its notes. The notes acting as samvádi in these tunes are पा and गी and these are at the intervals of 13 and 9 shrutis from सा.

This demonstrates the folly of discarding shrutis or gráma of the old Indian music, on which we have seen so far the whole structure of music is founded. If the foundation is discarded, the structure is bound to be unstable and to fall. Dissensions and differences of opinion would arise, which it would not be possible to settle, as there would be nothing to guide us, and in fact all scientific investigation would be impossible if the really scientific foundations laid by our old music-makers are ridiculed and discarded.

Chapter IX

TUNES

Vakra or oblique notes and tunes Tunes with 7 6 or 5 notes Murchhanas Possible number of tunes Ample scope for addition of tunes

IN Chapter VII we have found out the possible number of scales known as Janaka melas from which ragas are derived or, to say more correctly, the notes of which form the basis of the several ragas or tunes We have seen there could be 22 janaka melas If we substitute न for ना in the uttarangas to be used with the purvangas containing धो, which it was shown in Chapter VIII has good affinity for न and none for ना, we could have three more such scales with the uttaranga प धा न सं प धी न सं is not admissible as the interval between धी and न is only one shruti In this chapter it is intended to determine the possible number of tunes, and that in practical use

The process by which tunes are derived is again called Murchhana (मूर्च्छना), although here it has a somewhat different meaning from what it had been given when the process was used to obtain Vikrita swaras, and original melas or scales [*vide* Chapter VI] Here it simply means modulation or raising and lowering of sounds in music so as to form melody. The rise or successive ascent of notes (*i.e*, going from a note of lower pitch to one of a higher pitch) is, as we have seen, called Árohana, and the fall or descent (*i.e.*, going the other way) is known as Avarohana in Indian music Every tune can be divided in two parts, one ascending and the other descending It may happen that before reaching the extreme limit we may have one or more turns, *e.g.* स री स गी म धी नी धी स. This makes the tune tortuous and it is called Vakra [वक्र meaning crooked or tortuous]. The note which gives the turn (री and नी in the above example) is also called Vakra, and it is conventionally held that the turning note belongs to the portion of the tune (Aroha or Avaroha) which follows it. री and नी, here, belong to Avarohana or descent portion because they each precede a lower note. Some of the notes may be left out in a tune, either in ascent or in descent, or in both, as प in the above example. Such notes are called Varjita [meaning left out].

It is almost universally accepted that to form a tune there must be at least five notes, although two tunes, Shri (श्री) and Malashri (मालश्री) are sometimes sung with four and three notes only, also Hindola (हिन्दोल) has only four notes in Arohana. There cannot, therefore, be more than two varjita notes in a tune or properly speaking in each of the two parts of a tune as it is possible the Arohana of a tune may have one set left out and the Avarohana another. A tune or part of a tune having all the seven notes (either Shuddha or Vikrita) is called Sampúrna (सम्पूर्ण, meaning complete), that with only six notes is called Shadava (षाडव from षष् or षट् meaning "six"), and that with only five notes is called Audava [औडव, from उडुव, meaning sky or Akasha which, being the fifth of the five divisions of matter stands for the number five].

The process of evolving tunes from the Janaka melas by employing the full or a smaller number of notes, as above, in both the Arohana and Avarohana portions is called Murchhana. It divides itself into the following nine classes —

No. 1.—Sampúrna-Sampúrna (संपूर्ण संपूर्ण), *i.e.*, having all the seven notes in both ascent and descent ;

No. 2.—Sampúrna-Shàdva (सं. षाडव), having seven notes in ascent and six in descent ;

No. 3.—Samp-Audava (सं. औडव), having seven notes in ascent and five in descent;

No 4.—Ṣhádava Sampúrna (षाडव संपूर्ण), having six notes in ascent and seven in descont ;

No 5.—Shád Shadva (षा—षाडव) with six notes in ascent and six in descent ;

No. 6.—Shád Audava (षा—औडव) with six notes in ascent and five in descent :

No. 7.—Audava Sampúrna (औडव संपूर्ण) with five notes in ascent and seven in descent ;

No. 8 —Audava-Shàdava (औडव षाडव) with five notes in ascent and six in descent ; and

No. 9.—Audava Audava (औ औडव) with five notes in ascent and five in descent

Not taking into account the vakra or oblique tunes that may be formed, these nine classes of Murchhanás can evolve the following number of tunes from each of the Janaka melas [parent scales] :

No 1 Murchhana will give one tune

No 2 will give six, as स cannot be left out

No 3 When two notes are left out they almost invariably form a Samvadi pair There are a few exceptions which need not be considered in this general calculation Leaving those with स, we have only five Samvadi pairs, *viz*, Rishabha Dhaivata, Rishabha Panchama, Gándhára Dhaivata, Gandhára Nisháda and Madhyama Nisháda This murchhaná therefore gives five tunes

No 4 will give six tunes, like No 2

No 5 Arohana has six variations and each can have three corresponding variations in Avarohana (*i e*, one identical note and two samvadis) except प and म which can have only two, because स one of their Samvadis can not be left out There can therefore be 6×3 2 or 16 tunes under this murchhana

No 6 As said under No 3, Avarohana can have only five pairs, and for each pair there can be two varjita notes in Arohana Hence this murchhana gives 5 x 2 or 10 tunes

No 7 gives five tunes, like No 3

No. 8 gives ten tunes, like No. 6.

No. 9. There being five pairs of samvádis in each of the two parts, this murchhaná will give 5 × 5 or 25 tunes

By this process of murchhanas we thus get 84 tunes for each Janaka mela, or say 90 tunes taking into account vakra or oblique tunes and those not covered by the data above As we have 25 possible scales, including the three formed by introducing a new note न, the total number of tunes comes to 90 × 25 or 2,250. The 25 scales differ from each other very slightly, so there will be a lot of overlapping of the tunes For instance, in the case of scales 1 and 2 (*vide* statement on page 69) which differ only in Gándhàra the tunes without this note Gàndhàra will all be common. We can not therefore count upon more than say 2,000 tunes in all.

This number is capable of increase to a certain extent, as different tunes are formed by adopting different Vádi notes, although the general scale may remain the same. On the other hand, tunes for being melodious require appropriate notes following each other, and any and every combination will not do. There is besides another factor which tends to reduce the number considerably The character of a tune is generally distinguishable in the Arohana (ascent) and the Avarohana portion only supplements or embellishes it A Sampurna arohana does not therefore generally admit of a Shadava or Audava avarohana, which means that there are very few, if any, tunes coming under the classes Sampurna Shadava and Sampurna Audava Similarly Shadava arohana may have a Sampurna or a Shadava avarohana, but hardly an Audava avarohana This almost nullifies the murchhanas Nos 2, 3 and 6, or takes away about $\frac{1}{4}$ of the total number of tunes, thus leaving only about 1,500, tunes in all It is rather strange that Chatura Pandita in his *Laksha Sangita*, ignoring all the restrictions and overlappings noted above, and taking the old 72 scales of Venkateshwara, gives the number of possible tunes as 34,848 He however says the number of good ragas is limited by the fact that they have to be pleasing

The number of tunes in Hindustani music at present in use is near about 200 We could not expect anything better after centuries of neglect of the art by the intelligentsia, which art, since the later Mohammedan period till very recently, has been entirely in the hands generally of illiterate professionals. It may however be said to their credit that most of the tunes and essentials of the system have been well preserved by them, even though the principles leading to those essentials have been forgotten An endeavour has been made in this treatise to establish these principles, in order that the essentials of the system preserved so far may not be discarded as baseless and disregarded in any additions that may be made in this direction. We have seen there is still a lot of room for any number of new tunes being added.

The conduct of life is fast changing in India, new perceptions, new emotions and new ideas, amalgamating East and West, are displacing the old perceptions, emotions and ideas. Music will also have to shape itself to conform to the new state of things. It will be seen that our foundations are wide enough to take the new structure, without any change in the system.

Chapter X

RAGAS OR MELODIOUS TUNES

Raga defined Its arrangement. Tanas Alankaras Ban on Tivra Madhyama

THE word used for a tune in Indian music is *Raga* (राग) A raga is thus defined in *Sangita Darpana*

'योय ध्वनि विशेषस्तु स्वर वर्ण विभूषित ।
रजको जन चित्ताना स राग कथ्यते बुधै ॥"

i e, a raga is spoken of by learned men as that which is embellished with the colour of musical notes, has its separate tune and import, and is pleasing to the mind

Any and every tune cannot therefore be called a raga, which must have the following distinctive features

(*i*) The notes composing it should be so arranged as to be melodious, (*ii*) any adjunct to it *e g*, a drone or a subordinate musical accompaniment, either instrumental or vocal, must be in harmony with it, (*iii*) it should be clearly distinguishable from other rágas. In Indian music, each rága has been given a name; (iv) Its tune may be capable of conveying a particular emotion or idea; (v) It should be sung at a time when the state of mind conforms with its import, as otherwise it will not be pleasing.

There is another thing which is very essential for music, although not indispensible for rágas, as distinct from songs. It is the rhythm or keeping time, known as Tála (ताल) in Indian music

Coming first to the melodious arrangement of notes, we have in Chapter VIII investigated what affinity each note bears with the others. We have seen that Samvádis and Anuvadis are more concordant than others, and also have found out which of the pairs form good combinations and which not. The bad combinations noted there cannot be used when the component parts are meant to be sounded together, but there is no objection to using them as adjacent notes, as parts of a bigger scheme because they do bear concordant relations with each other For adjacent couples the bigger the intervals the more vigorous the combination, *e. g*, shruti interval is more vigorous than a 6 shruti one 6 shruti better than 5 shruti, and so on We cannot however have the same interval repeated successively as it will be monotonous, and it is better to rise or fall with easy steps Smaller and bigger intervals have therefore to be mixed up to make a tune melodious The intervals in the sargams of the following common tunes will illustrate the point —

Bhairava—

Intervals between स and स̅ 2, 4 3 4 2 4 3 = 22 Shrutis

Bhairva—

Intervals between स and स 2, 5 2 4 2 5, 2 = 22 Shrutis

Malakosha -

Intervals between स and स̅ 6 3 6 4 3 = 22 Shrutis

Samvadis (9—13 shrutis) or octaves (22 shrutis) are also used as adjacent notes occasionally, but not very often (the latter less often than the former) as Indian music approaches its notes by easier steps, not by leaps This is done only in the way of relief from successive shorter intervals It is known as 'Chhúta" (छूट) meaning release or relief An 8 shruti interval is bad and rarely used, except that म धी म is sometimes used, but surely म ध म would be better, and it is due to the absence of ध from our present gamut that म धी न has been allowed.

The whole character of a tune cannot very well be depicted in all cases in one stretch from स to स̄, and one or more turns have to be taken, which produce Vakra notes and make the tune itself more or less Vakra, as noticed already in the previous chapter. This is effected by introducing what is called a Tána [तान]. Tána (from the root तन्, to spread) is defined as that which is used to expand a rága, and consists of a certain number of the notes put in different orders. It is one of the things about which there seems to be a muddle. Every one of the writers on music seems to consider it of great importance to give the possible number of Tánas, *i.e.*, ⌊7 or 5040 for seven notes, ⌊6 or 720 for six notes, ⌊5 or 120 for five, ⌊4 or 24 for four, ⌊3 or 6 for three, 2 for two notes and 1 for one note for each múrchhaná, without any consideration whatever for overlappings and to explain how they could be worked out. And yet the real use of so many tánas has been admitted as not being quite clear. It has been said in one place that out of these only 84 are used for expansion of múrchhanás or rágas.

Tánas are of two kinds, Shuddha and Kúta [कूट—illusive, not straight] A Shuddha tana has all its notes in the natural order, either in ascent or in descent, as रिगम and मगरि are Shuddha tanas of the three notes, रि, ग, and म A Kúta tána has not got its notes in the correct order रिमग गरिम, गमरि, and मरिग, are Kúta tánas of the same three notes

Sarraya i Ishrat, an Urdu book written in 1874, says that a tana consists of only four notes or less, and that any greater number of notes will take it to the category of a rága This view seems to be correct The book gives the number of Kúta tanas as 52, but not how the figure was arrived at Tánasen recognised 49 Kúta tanas

The actual number of tanas between प and स̄ from combinations of 2, 3 and 4 notes comes, after eliminating the overlappings, to 60 altogether, divided as follows —

Shuddha tanas original múrchhana, 1, two-note combinations, 5, three note combinations, 4, four note combinations 3 Kúta tánas three note combinations, 8, four note combinations, 39 From the definition there can be no Kuta tanas for two note combinations, and for ordinary purposes of forming ragas, tanas of more than four notes are not required

The tánas of two and three notes give Vakra swaras, and those of three and four notes Vakra rágas However a rága is not generally called so, unless almost the whole of its Arohana or Avarohana takes a tortuous character

For embellishment, repetitions of the notes that enhance the melodiousness of a rága are introduced. This is generally done through the tánas, both Shuddha and Kúta. The repetition is effected by the processes known as (1) Sphurana (स्फुरण = quivering, or using the notes twice, (2) Tripu (त्रिपु) or using them thrice; (3) Kampana (कंपन = trembling or shaking), in which the notes are repeated several times but with shorter durations, (4) Andolana (अन्दोलन = swinging), in which notes are repeated so that one ot a longer duration comes between those of shorter durations, *e.g.*, स स सा स, मपाप, म गा ग; (5) Áhati (आहति = rolling), in which similar tánas of ascending notes follow in succession, *e.g*, सरिग, रिगम, गमप; and (6) Pratyáhati (प्रत्याहति), in which similar tánas of descending notes follow in succession, *e g.*, स नि, निध, धप. The tánas used in this way are called alankáras (अलंकार := an ornament) in Indian music. A good number (over 60) of these has been composed and mentioned in the old books, and each given a name.

Alankaras were considered a necessity, as they are at present also, for good music Bharata says, "a song without an alankara is like a night without moon, a river without water, a creeper without flowers, and a woman without ornaments" A few simple ones are noted below with their names, the full number can be seen in any of the old granthas (ग्रन्था), *Sangita Parijatak* or *Sangita Darpana* for instance or in the Urdu book *Maarifun Nagmat* by Mohammed Nawab Ali Khan Sahib of Sitapur

Bhadra—स रि स, रि ग रि ग म ग, -

Nanda—स स रि रि सस, रि रि ग ग रि रि, -

Jita—स ग रि स, रि मग रि,

Bhala—स ग रि म म ग रिस, रि म ग प प म ग रि

Bindu—सस स रि, रि रि रि ग, - -

Trivarna—स रि ग ग ग, रि ग म म म, - -

Akshepa—स रि ग, रि ग म, ग म प,

Krama—स रि रि ग ग म, रि ग ग म म प

Kokila—स रि ग स रि ग म, रि ग म रि ग म प,

Mahavajra—स रि ग रि स रि ग म, रि ग म ग रिग म प,

Mandradi—स रि ग म म ग रिस स रि ग रि स रि ग म,
रि ग म प प म ग रि रि गम ग रि ग म प,

According to the ascent or descent of the notes Alankaras are divided into four classes called Varnas [वर्ण] When the notes are ascending, the Alankara is called Arohi Varna, when descending it is called Avarohi Varna, when the notes are both ascending and descending, it is called Sanchárí (संचारी = changeable); when the notes return to the original note from which the start was made or when there are repetitions the Alankára is called Sthái Varna [स्थाई = standing]

The Alankáras have shuddha or vikrita swaras according to the rágas they are used in Also the Varjita swaras in a rága must be left out in its alankára also. In the present-day music, these alankáras are called Paltá, Tána or Tora when played on a musical instrument, when sung with the initials of the notes (स, रि, ग etc.) they are called Sargams (or Tánas of the Sargam); and when only the sound of the notes is uttered, leaving out the initials, they form what is called an álapam (आलापम्) The last two are peculiar to the Indian music, and make the rága very pleasing and highly artistic

Each rága is supposed to have its vádí and samvàdí notes, which mostly determine its import. These are either more frequently used than other notes, or used in such a way as to be prominent. Next to these, are their Anuvádís, and then the Nirvadís. Vivádís are to be the least employed and, if likely to affect the character of the tune, to be altogether avoided. If used at all they might come in Avarohana, not in Arohana. The Samvádís, Anuvádís etc. for each note have been worked out in Chapter VIII.

It would not be out of place to note down a tune to illustrate what has been said above, and to show how music masters arrange their compositions It has been taken from a song, in the tune known as *Hansa Nārāyan* (हस नारायण) in Purví mela, composed by Chatura Pandita, the author of *Laksha Sangita*, and given in Ma árifun Nagmát

                                                  गो
Notes———स रा गी मी प प प प मी गो मी प मी गी रा स

Intervals— 2 5 4 2 – – – 2 4 4 2 2 4 5 2 shrutis

Notes———स रा गी रा स स प प मी गी मी रा गी रा रा स

Intervals— 2 5 5 2 – 13 – 2 4 4 9 5 5 – 2 shrutis.

The following things may be noted —

(1) Intervals from 2 to 5 shrutis have been mixed up

(2) These have been relieved in two places by introducing samvadi intervals of 13 and 9 shrutis

(3) There is no interval of 8 shrutis nor any couple of adjacent intervals aggregating to 8 shrutis

(4) There is a uniformity in diversity in both the parts of the song noted above The beginning and end in each case are reversals of each other

(5) रा गी रा, मी गी मी, स रा गी रा स are the alankaras introduced

(6) स and प are noted in the book as Vadi and Sámvádi but the way in which स has been used does hardly warrant for it the character of a Vadí प too although used rather profusely does not peculiarise the tune, which is, as will be seen done by मी and रा The tune *Hansa Narayana* is Audava shadava, in which धा is entirely to be left out and नी used in avarohana only धा, and नी are not vivadís of either स or प but are their anuvadis They are Vivadis of मी and रा It therefore appears more correct to take मी and रा as Vadí

and Samvádí in the tune *Hansa Náráyana* than taking स and प. There seems to be a reluctance on the part of the post-Ratnákara musicians to make मी as Vádí due perhaps to the fact that स is now the chief note and मी is not in good concordant relation with it; but this is not a good reason, for मी is not in good relation with स either, but there is no objection to taking it as Vádí. For the same reason perhaps नी, which is a samvadi of मी has also been banned. This is a matter again for the experts to look into. The campaign against untouchability should also be extended to music to increase the utility of the banned swaras like मी, नी, etc.

In depriving मी of its Vádísm, it is necessary to get the Vádí-place taken by some other note, and, for this purpose, in the tunes which particularly require the use of मी, स and प or स and म are prolonged in their use. This is perhaps the case with the tune *Hansa Náráyan* too.

Chapter XI

RHYTHM OR TIMING

Tala defined, Matras and their divisions, difference with European timing Old Jati talas, Present talas and their derivation from old talas Sama and Vishama graha

THE element of time is as essential to music as to any other affair of the world As a regular succession of sound vibrations is necessary to make the sound musical, as a regular coincidence of the vibrations of musical notes makes these notes concordant, as an appropriate blending of concordant notes at proper intervals is required to create melody, so for good music it is essential that the component melodious pieces should follow each other at regular and appropriate intervals of time This keeping of time was effected in India by clapping of the hands, and was hence called Tala [ताल clapping of hands, from तल a palm of the hand] The practice is still in vogue

The instruments in use for the purpose are Pakhavaja Mridanga, Tablá etc, which not only keep time but their sweet sounds, and parans and

Gamaks (tánas) enhance the quality of music. Their basis of play however, is the original tála, the rules of which govern them also.

The interval between two claps or strokes, which is termed a laghu (लघु=small), is governed by two considerations. (1) The smallest interval should be such that the hand may not get tired in the course of one rága or song, and (2) the other extremity should be in conformity with its function of keeping time, for if the interval be too big, the object would be lost. For the first, it was thought that the time taken by a beat of the pulse of a fairly-healthy man is the proper smallest interval and, for the second, about three times this interval. These limits cannot evidently be very hard and fast.

The interval is also considered in another way, *viz.*, in terms of syllabic instants, called mátrás [मात्रा] A matra is taken as the shortest time in which a syllable could be properly pronounced It was taken and perhaps correctly, that about three syllables could well be pronounced during one beat of the pulse Therefore a laghu ranges from 3 to 9 mátras. Its usual value, unless specifically mentioned otherwise, is taken as 4 mátrás, and as such the following are its sub-divisions and multiples.

8 Kshanas (क्षण)=1 lava लव, 8 lavas=1 Kàshtha काष्ठा 8 Kashthas=1 nimisha (निमिष), 8 nimishas = 1 Kala (कला), 4 kalas=anudruta (अनुद्रुत) or anu or viráma (विराम), 2 anus=1 druta (द्रुत), 2 drutas=1 laghu (लघु) 2 laghus=1 guru (गुरु), 3 laghus=1 pluta (प्लुत) and 4 laghus=1 Kakapada [काकपद]

An anu or virama is thus equal to one matra and denoted by the sign U, a druta=2 matras with its sign O, a laghu=4 matras (unless specifically mentioned to have other values) and has the sign=1 a guru=8 matras with its sign S, a pluta =12 mátrás with sign ३, and a kakapada=16 matras with sign + Three matras are denoted by a combination of Viráma and druta as ŏ, and 5 matras by a combination of Virama and laghu as ĭ

As is natural there is a lot of difference of opinions as to the time of a matra, but the exact time is not of any great consequence and need not worry us What is necessary to understand is the values of laghu with reference to matras as noted above On the time taken by a matra however, depends the quick or slow singing of a song which is denoted by the term Laya [लय=motion, from the root लय् to move] When quick, it is called Druta laya [द्रुत=quick], when slow it is called Vilambita laya (विलम्बित=retarded), the ordinary one being known as Madhya Laya [मध्य=middle]

The approximate European equivalent to a mátrá is half a crotchet, which makes the ordinary laghu as equal to a minim, the European subdivisions being as follows, 1 semibreve,=2 minims = 4 crotchets=8 quavers=16 semiquavers =32 demi-semi-quavers. There is in this respect a little difference in the European and Indian systems. While the European semibreve and its sub-divisions represent the time for which a particular note is sounded, the Indian laghu etc show the interval between two strokes of the tála, without any reference to the notes. The notes may of course be fitted in as desired by the singer within the interval, but the tála has been treated by the Indian musicians independently of notes and tunes.

As has been said above the convenient interval between tàla strokes is a laghu ranging from 3 to 9 mátrás. Smaller intervals of one and two mátrás and bigger ones of more than 9 mátrás were also in vogue in the old music, but generally mixed up with the standard laghu interval. These were used in the playing of pakhávaja. In the current Indian music a two mátra interval is the only exception.

Several intervals, either of similar or different durations combine to form what is called a tàla or measure for the songs or parts thereof In reference to the rhythmic instruments, pakhávaja, tabla etc the measure is called theka [ठेका=a fixed arrangement] The combinations are written in the notations of the intervals given above For instance, OIU represents a tala of 7 matras containing three strokes, the first of 2 matras the second of 4 and the third of one matra The notation is known as Anga (अंग) or body of the tala as it shows its composition

The old music makers devised seven talas known as Jati talas (जाति=class or species) from which all the other talas were derived These are as follows

Number	Names of the talas	Notation or Anga	No of matras taking laghu of 4 matras	No of strokes	Possible modifications
1	Ekatala [एकताल]	I	4	1	
3	Rupaka [रूपक]	OI	2+4=6	2	IO
3	Jhampa [झम्प]	IUO	4+1+2=7	3	UOI OIU
4	Triputa [त्रिपुट]	IOO	4+2+2=8	3	OOI OIO
5	Mathya In order [मठ्य]	IOI	4+2+4=10	3	IIO IIO

Number	Names of the talas	Notation or Anga	No of matras taking laghu of 4 matras	No. of strokes	Possible modifications
6	Atha [अठ]	IIOO	4+4+2+2=12	4	IOOI, OOII, OIIO
7	Dhruva [ध्रुव]	IOII	4+2+4+4=14	4	OIII, IIIO, IIOI

By changing the value of laghu to 3, 5, 4, and 9 mátrás 28 more tálas were obtained. Each of these 35 tálas was given a name The laghu was not given the value 6 or 8 mátrás perhaps because these were doubles of 3 and 4. Some tálas were also obtained by repeating one or the other of the small talas. The longest tála that could be obtained from these Jati Talas without repetition was of 29 matras, i.e dhruva with the laghu of 9 mátrás but ordinarily tálas of more than 16 mátrás were perhaps of rare use In the time of Shárngdeva, however, we find talas of much greater length, reaching as much as 60 or 70 mátrás but these were all meant for pakhávaja its parans and tànas and not for keeping time with hands. The following table gives tálas up to 16 mátrás as worked out from the usual forms of Játi tálas.

Table of Talas

No	Tála Matras	Jati talas with notation							Repetitions		
		I Ek tala 1	II Rupaka 01	III Jhampa 1U0	IV Triputa 100	V Mathya 101	VI Atta 1100	VII Dhruva 1011	VIII Twice	IX 3 times	X 4 times
1	3	3	—	—	—	—	—	—	—	—	—
2	4	4	—	—	—	—	—	—	—	—	—
3	5	5	2+3	—	—	—	—	—	—	—	—
4	6	—	2+4	3+1+2	—	—	—	—	No 1		—
5	7	7	2+5	4+1+2	3+2+2	—	—	—	—	—	—
6	8	—	—	5+1+2	4+2+2	3+2+3	—	—	No 2	—	—
7	9	9	2+7	—	3+2+3	—	—	—	—	No 1	—
8	10	—	—	7+1+2		4+2+4	3+3+2+2	—	No 3	—	—

No.	Tála matras.	I Ek-tala. 1	II Rupaka, 01	III Jhampa. 1U0	IV Triputa. 100	V Mathya. 101	VI Atha. 1100	VII Dhruva 1011	VIII Twice	IX 3 times.	X 4 times
		Játi tálas with notation.							Repetitions.		
9	11	—	2+9	—	7+2+2	—	—	3+2+3+3	—	—	—
10	12	—	—	9+1+2	—	5+2+5	4+4+2+2	—	No.4	No.2	No.1
11	13	—	—	—	9+2+2	—	—	—	—	—	—
12	14	—	—	—	—	—	5+5+2+2	4+2+4+4	No.5	—	—
13	15	—	—	—	—	—	—	—	—	No 3	
14	16	—	—	—	—	7+2+7	—	—	No 6	—	No.2

Each tala had, as is the case now also, one of the strokes on which more stress was given than the others, and for the sake of contrast to make it more prominent the stroke, or more correctly speaking the mátrá, directly opposite was given the least stress The stroke following the stressed stroke is also sometimes treated in the same way to give prominence to the latter The stress thus brought on a stroke was [also now called Sama [सम meaning composure after agitation] The strokes with little or no stress are now known as Khálí (empty), the old name for which was Nishabda [नि : शब्द्—without sound], all the other strokes being called Sashabda [with sound] In pakhávaja, tablá, etc , the nishabda stroke is without a stroke on the left-hand side of the instrument which gives the full or *thun* sound In some cases the instruments cease to play for a nishabda stroke, the player keeping the time in his mind only

In the present day music, tála strokes of more than four matrás or less than two mátras are not generally used, so the longer strokes of the old talas have been split up in many cases, the second part being given a Khálí and the old one mátra stroke is joined to the preceding or the following stroke

The following table gives the important tálas in current use, with their composition and the corresponding old játi tálas from which they have been derived. The sama and khali points have also been indicated.

No	Name of the Tala	No of strokes with matras showing the Sama marked × showing the Khali marked 0 and other strokes marked (1), (2) (3) &c	Corresponding old old jati tala with its anga and name Reference given to table p 111 112	Remarks
1	Ektala	× 0 (2) 0 (3) (4) 3 + 2 + 3 + + 2 + 2 = 12 Matras	Ektala (1) of two matra laghu called Ektala by Sharngdeva repeated six times	Here the laghu has been taken of two matras which was not contemplated in Jatis talas but Sharngdeva has taken it in this case The last stroke has not been given Khali to give greater stress to the Sama
2	Dadra	× (2) 3 + 3 — 6 Matras	Ektala (1) of 3 matras called shuddha tala repeated twice × vide [4 VIII]	

No.	Name of the Tala.	Number of strokes with matras showing the Sama marked ×, the Khali marked O, and other strokes marked (1), (2), (3), etc.	Corresponding old jati tala with its anga and name. Reference given to table p. 111, 112	Remarks
3	Khemtá	× (2) 0 (3) 3+3+3+3=12 Matras.	Ektala(1)of three matras called shuddha tala repeated four times *vide* [10X]	
	Kaharvá ...	× (2) 4+4=8 Matras.	Ektala (1) of four matras, called Manatala taken twice, *vide* [6VIII.]	

5	Titálá	—	× (3) 0 (1) 1+4+4+4—16 Matras	Ektala (1) of four matras called Manatala repeated four times vide [14X]	
6	Talwárá		Do	—	Same as Titala differing only in strokes of the Tabla
7	Punjábi theká		Do		Do
8	Rūpaka		(1) (2) × 2+2+3=7 Matras	Rupakatala, (O1) of seven matras called kala tala, vide [5II]	The five matra laghu has been split up the second part of three matras although having the Sama is played as Khali in Pakhavaja and Tabla.

No.	Name of the Tala.	Number of strokes with matras showing the Sama marked ×, showing the Khali marked O, and other strokes marked (1), (2), (3) etc.	Corresponding old jati tala with its anga and name, Reference given to table p. 111-112	Remarks.
9	Jhaptálá ...	× (2) 0 (3) 2+3+2+3=10 Matras	Jhampa tála (OIU) of ten matras, known as Swaratála, vide [S III].	The seven-matra laghu has been split up into 3+2+2, and virama combined with the last two matras to give three matras. It could also be taken as the Rupaka of five matras [3 II] taken twice.

10	Jhumrá	(1) × (3)0 4+3+4+3—14 Matras	Jhampa tàla(1UO) of seven matras called madhura tala taken twice *vide* [12 VIII]	The viráma has been amalgamated with the following druta and the combined stroke given sama in one case and khali in the other
11	Chàchar	Do.		Same as Jhumra differing only in tabla strokes and played a bit quicker
12	Tivrá ...	(1) (2) × 3+2+3—7 Matras	Triputa tála (OO1) of seven matra called shankha tála *vide* [5IV]	

No.	Name of Tala.	No. of strokes with matras. showing the same marked ×, Khali marked O, and others strokes marked (1) (2), etc.	Corresponding old jati tala with its anga and name. Reference given to table p. 111-112	Remarks.
13	Pashtu	× (2) (3) 3 + 2 + 2 = 7 Matras	Triputa tàla(100) of seven Matras, called. Shankha tàla, *vide* [5 IV].	Same as Tivra, differing only in the tabla strokes and played more vilambita
14	Sùl or Sùl Fàkhta	× 0 (2) 0 (3) 2 + 2 + 2 + 2 + 2 = 10 Matras	Mathya tála(110) of ten Matras, known as Sama tàla, *vide* [8V]	The two laghus have been split up to supply Khalis.
15	Dhamár ...	× 0 (2) 0 (3) (4) 3 + 2 + 3 + 2 + 2 + 2 = 14 Matras	Atha tala (1100) of fourteen mat-	The two laghus of five matras have

			ras called Vodatala *vide* [13 VI]	been split up to supply Khalis The last druta is played as Khali in tabla
16	Chautâlâ or Dhrupada	× 0 (2) 0 (3) (4) 1+2+2+2+2+2=12 Matras	Atha tala (IIOO) of twelve Matras called Lokha tala, *vide* [10 VI]	The two laghus have been split up to supply khalis
17	Ará Chautala	× (2) 0(3) 0 (4) 2+2+2+2+2+4=14 Matras	Dhruva tàla (OIII) of fourteen Matras known as Shikhara tala *vide* [12 VII]	Two of the laghus have been split up to provide khalis

NOTE. - It appears the names of Nos. 16 and 17 have been inter-changed, as the derivative Jati tálas suggest Ara for No 16 and Dhruva for 17

From the Játi tàlas it will be seen that only four strokes were originally comtemplated, and it was by splitting some of the strokes that in the present music we have more than four strokes, but in these cases the excess goes as Kháli. Below are given a few tálas which have more than four strokes. These were devised by old music-makers like Sharngdeva and others, and are still used, though rarely.

	Name of Tála	Anga or strokes with Matras	Remarks
1	Gaja Jhampá tála	S000U=15 Matras	In the present music the Guru is broken up into 4+1 and the viráma added to the preceding druta so that the present anga is × 0 (2) (3) (4) 4+1+2+2+3
2	Chakra tála	I000I00I0I=[illegible] Matras	The Sama is on the first laghu and Khali on the last
3	Chandra Shekhara or Shekhara tála	0II00I00II=30 Matra	This tála a bit modified is known as Savara or Savári in the present music its anga being 8+[illegible]+8+6
4	Farodast	I000I=14 Matras	The present anga is × o (2) (3) (4) o 2+2+2+2+2+4 It is said to have been devised by Amir Khusru

The strokes of pakhavaja or tablá are fitted in accordance with the strokes of the tála as noted above. Tánas have also been composed for these instruments which, however lengthy, must in the end come to the particular tála, the samas of the two coinciding.

The coincidence is known as Graha [ग्रह= grasp, or perhaps the softened prákrita form of ग्रन्थ=a tie or knot] When the two samas coincide regularly, it is called a sama graha (सम=equal), otherwise it is a Vishama graha [विषम=irregular]. The latter is of two kinds: (1) Atíta in which the sama of the instrument comes after that of the real tála, and (2) anágata, in which it precedes the sama of the tála. In the one case, the speed of the instrument has to be quickened, and in the other it is to be slackened in order that the next samas may coincide with the sama of the tála.

The rágas or songs, except in very special cases when emotions have to be expressed, have to follow one or the other of the tálas In order that a rága may be vigorous and pleasing, the position of its sama should be occupied by the vádi or samvádi swaras, and these should form a sama graha with the sama of the tála. When tánas are taken, the graha may sometimes be vishama to coincide later as explained above But it is not always considered necessary to have this coincidence in which cases however the distances must remain uniform throughout

In some cases more talas than one are used, particularly, in the old Indian music, two or three talas were mixed up in the sort of songs known as Prabandha To go from one tala to another particular care had to be taken so that the point of change might not be distinguished as abrupt This could be effected by quickening or slackening the layas of the adjacent talas so as to get them blended together

The laya of a raga or song is determined by its subject and import, a grave and solemn or plaintive raga requires Vilambita laya that expressing sport, ridicule, or merriment, requires Druta laya, the Madhya laya being used for ordinary songs

Below is given a raga, by way of illustration, to show its tála and the corresponding tabla strokes The tune is Imana with sama on the first syllable, or rather druta, the tála being Chautála

Song — भ ज । म न । श्री ह् । रा आ । म ना । श्या म ।
सु ख । स म् । प ति । दु ह् । क धा । श्या म ।

Tune, *Imana*—नीधी। प मी। गी मी। प प। मी गी। नी गी।
गोरी। गी मी। प मी। री गी। री नी। री स।
× ० (२) ० (३) (४)
Tála Chautálá—२। २। २। २। २। २।
Tablà Strokes—। dhá dhá। tin ná। kit dhá। dhin ná। kit tik। gid gin।

If the song be sung in the tune *Bhairavi*, the notes will be as below —

प प। धा प। गा गा। म म। गा ग। स स।
ना स। गा गा। म म। ना धा। प धा। प गा।

The sama in this case shifts to the seventh syllable or fourth druta, so the sama of the tabla stroke (dhá-dhá) must be brought here to have the sama graha, otherwise the graha will be vishama, and not quite pleasant.

Chapter XII

HARMONY

Harmony defined. Forgotten in India. Three kinds of Harmony in Indian Music

WHEN two or more concordant notes are sounded together, they form what is called Harmony. The Indian word for harmony is Laya (लय = union, fusion, from the root ली=to adhere, to vanish) being in this sense different from the word laya, used for the slow or quick motion of a tune in the previous chapter. In chapter VIII the relation of each note with others was investigated and it was found that pairs of notes with 9—13 shruti intervals, known as samvádis and 6—16 and 7—15 shruti intervals, *i.e.*, anuvadis, were concordant. An octave of a note is of course concordant to the latter. In European music the notes with 5—17 shruti intervals are also taken as concordant.

For harmony, when a tune is played, its salient and prominent points are supplemented by sounding the harmonical notes as mentioned above, whereby the sweetness of music is largely en hanced. The latter notes form a tune in themselves which the ear is capable of hearing distinctly separately from the main tune, as also at the same time in combination with it so that the effect is exceedingly pleasing. It is not necessary that each note of the harmony tune should be concordant with the corresponding notes of the main tune Discords are sometimes introduced, as a contrast, to increase the value of the concords The harmony tune is generally played in a lower octave or sthána.

The art of harmony was well developed by the old Indian musicians, but it has become almost extinct at the present day All that we see of it is the sounding with music of drones representing the main note, shadja and its fifth, which provide harmony of a sort The chief instrument for this purpose is the Tambura, which has three wires representing Shadja, and one representing Panchama. The Víná, the Sitár, the Sarangi, and other similar instruments have also extra wires or strings tuned to Shadja, Panchama etc, which resonate and enhance the volume of music. The Tábla is also tuned with Shadja, or sometimes with other notes if desired by the singer.

Three kinds of harmony seem to have been practised in India, *viz.*, Swara laya (स्वर लय),

Ansha laya (अंश=a part) and Anyonya laya [अन्योन्य=mutual] Swara laya is the harmony provided by the individual notes as in the case of drones and their samvádí and anuváda swaras The arrangement of the uttaranga being exactly the fifth of the purvánga in the Indian scale of music has the peculiar advantage of providing harmony if desired, for a tune may be played in the ordinary manner and it may, at the same time, be played on the uttaranga of a lower sthána, and the two will be in exact harmony They will have what may be called shadja panchama bhava [भाव=state]

In Indian music the sthái (स्थाई=anything permanent) of a song or raga, which shows its full tune with all the necessary notes correctly arranged, is generally divided into two or more parts or ansha These are in the same tala and used to be in the compositions of music masters, generally so arranged that if played together they were in harmony with each other Thus if one instrument plays the raga from the beginning and the other at the same time starts from say the second part in a lower octave the two instruments will be playing in harmony This is Ansha laya As one part will be following the other without actually overtaking it, it may be

9

termed Brahmoshá Bháva [अषा + उषा, *i.e*, the state of the sun following the dawn without being able to catch it]. It is called a fugue in European music. The sthái of the tune *Hansa Narayana* given in Chapter X (page 101) and those of the tunes *Iman* and *Bhairavi* given in the last chapter will be found with their parts to form fugues very nearly. This is shown below :—

(1) Hansa Narayan 1st part	स	रा	गी	मी	प	प	प	प	मी	गी	गी मो	प	मी	गी	रा	स
2nd part	स	रा	गी	रा	स	स	प	प	मी	गी	मी	रा	गी	रा	रा	स
Relation of the notes in Shrutis	0/22	0/22	c/22	9/13	9/13	9/13	0/22	0/22	0/22	0/22	c/22	11/11	4/18	5/17	0/22	0/22
Concord or discord	Concord											Discord			Concord	

(2) Iman 1st part	नी	धी	प	मी	गी	मी	प	प	मी	गी	गी	गी
2nd part	गी	री	गी	मी	प	मी	री	गी	रा	नी	री	स
Relation of Shruti	9/13	9/13	6/16	0/22	6/16	0/22	9/13	6/16	7/15	9/13	3/19	7/15
Concord or Discord	Concord										Discord	Concord

(3) Bhairavi, 1st part	प	प	धा	प	गा	गा	म	म	गा	रा	स	स
2nd part.	ना	स	गा	गा	म	म	ना	धा	प	धा	प	गा
Relation of notes in Shrutis	6/16	9/13	9/13	7/15	3/19	3/19	10/12	6/16	7/15	9/13	9/13	6/16
Concord or Discord.	Concord.				Discord.			Concord.				

The third kind of harmony (Anyonya laya, अन्योन्य लय) obtains between two ragas of different tunes This is known as counterpoint in European music and is a difficult composition The tunes must, of course be sung or played on the same tala The salient points of each of the tunes have to be concordant with those of the other The two tunes are heard separately, as also blended into one They have what may be called Pitipatni Bhava [पति=husband, पत्नी=wife] In India, for several rágas five or six such tunes as would harmonise with them were composed These latter were given feminine names and were known as wives or ragiuís of the former, which were called rágas The subject will be further treated in a subsequent chapter As has been said above, the art of harmony has been lost or given up, so that the ragas and raginis formerly connected in harmony are treated now as altogether separate tunes They have gradually undergone changes and alterations, and in many cases do not harmonise as they did before

Chapter XIII.

INDIAN RAGAS AND RAGINIS.

Ragas and Raginis how differentiated in different periods, Sargams of Ragas or tunes of current Indian music. Analysis of tunes by Music Experts.

WE shall now come to the different tunes in Indian music, and see how they are differentiated from each other. The points of difference, we have seen, are :—

(1) The Janaka mela to which the tune belongs, *vide* Chapter VII.

(2) The particular murchhana of that mela, *vide* Chapter IX.

(3) The existence or otherwise of vakra notes, *vide* Chapter X, and

(4) The Vadi and Samvadì swaras.

There were a few other points observed in the old music, *e.g.* Graha (ग्रह) or the note from which a tune commenced ; Nyása (न्यास) or the note on which a tune ended ; Tára, the note to which the tune extended in the tárasthána ; Mandra, the note to which the tune descended in the Mandrasthána, Bahutwa (बहुत्व) or mention of the note which was used most in a tune, and Alpatwa (अल्पत्व) or mention of the note which was used the least or was left out In the current music none of these, except the last and sometimes the first and second, is taken any notice of

One very important point of difference is the portion of the Saptaka, púrvánga or uttaranga, that is more impressive in a rága Some of the ragas show themselves in purvánga (स to म) and some in their uttaranga [प to सं] Also some are pleasing in their ascent (arohana) and some in descent [avarohana] The Púrvánga ragas are generally so in ascent and the Uttaránga ones in descent

The arrangement of the tunes has been different in different periods The oldest, and perhaps the natural one, was taking the gráma ragas first with their five divisions, Shuddha, Bhinna, Gauda, Vesara, and Sádharana, as already noticed, *vide* Chapter VI, and numbering 30 These being rather abstract scales had Bháshás (भाषा = speech or exposition), Vibháshás and Antarbhashas (alternatives) which were the tunes that showed them in a more practical way Then there were other rágas and uparágas and a lot of connected tunes known as rágángas, upángas, bhashángas, etc. Out of these ragas, bhashas, and angas, Shárngdeva, the author of *Sangita Ratnakara* mentioned 264, including the old tunes as well as those current in his time.

Among the post-Ratnákar writers there are some who take six rágas with five or six ráginis to each, ascribing the arrangement to older music-makers like Someshwara (or God Shiva), Bharata, and Hanumat. They go so far as to mention sons and daughters-in-law of each of the six rágas, which include almost all the tunes current in their time. It is not impossible that the old music-masters had some rágas for which they found out tunes allied to them in some way and called them their wives, but that all the rágas of Indian music could be included within groups of only six families is inconceivable, and a lot more of tunes must have been known to the old writers like Bharata etc. The rágas and their ráginis are not all the same with the different schools above, which shows that the tunes, although they retained the names, underwent many alterations in the course of time.

These rágas and ráginis have been ascribed forms of men and women in different attitudes and states of mind This no doubt had reference to the sentiments expressed by the different tunes, but as this aspect of music has long been lost, it is simply taken as poetic imagery and no heed is taken of it The tunes have now got modified and a lot of unauthorised inter polations has also been probably introduced, so that the descriptions given of the ráginis can hardly be indicated by their tunes The subject will be dealt with further later on

The rest of the post Ratnakara writers divide the rágas of their time under the several Janak melas (parent scales) whose notes form the basis of those rágas They are different in cases of different writers, showing the change that as was natural, went on gradually It is unneces sary to mention the janaka melas or tunes of these old writers as their notes are not, we have seen, all similar to ours Their shuddha rishabha and shuddha dhaivata are not, for instance, represented by any of our present notes, and but for the difference in these notes our scale Bhaírava would have been the same as the old Hejujji

The classification of the rágas at the present day is also done in the same way, *i e*, under the several janaka melas The Sanskrita book *Laksha*

Sangitam (लक्ष्य=current) of Chatura Pandita treats the subject very well giving almost all the important rágas and ráginis of the current Hindustani music with their points of difference and coincidence. Chatura Pandita has also composed Hindi songs, known as Lakshana gita, which are sung in the specific tunes, and give their special features, vádis, varjita swaras etc. The latter are also given in the small Sanskrita book *Ràga Chandriká* Every part of the country has in fact books, in its own dialect, on the subject, showing the particular notes used in each rága or rágini, its vadi, vivadi swaras etc. It is not therefore necessary to have all the matter repeated here, and only a few common current tunes are noted below under the different janaka-melas with their sargams and some important features.

Names of Janaka melas	Murchhana.	Names of the tunes	Sargams of the tunes	Purvanga or Uttaranga	Vadi and Samvadi	Remarks
1 Bhairavi	Sam Sam	Bhairavi	स, ना धा प, म, गा रा स ना स, गा म, प, धा ना स	n	स, म स, प, or धा गा	
	Aud Aud	Malakosh	ना स गा म धा ना स, स, ना धा म गा म, गा स	n	म स	रा and प are left out.
2 Vasanta Bhairavi	Sam Sam	Basanta Mukhari	स रा गी म, प धा ना स स धा प, ना धा प, धा प म, गी रा स	n	धा रा	
3 Bhairava	Do	Bhairava	रा स, धा नी स, गी म प, धा, प, म गी रा स	n	धा रा	रा is weak in Arohi

Names of Janaka melas.	Murchhana	Names of the tunes	Sargams of the tunes,	Purvanga or Uttaranga.	Vadi and Samvadi	Remarks,
Bhairava (*contd*)	Sam Sam	Prabháta	म गी, रा स, धा नी स, गी, म धा प म, म गी रा गी म मी	u	म स	Both Madhyamas used and close together.
	Sam Sam	Kalingrà	नी स, रा गी म, गी म प धा, प धा नी धा प, गी म, गी रा स	u	गी नी	
	Aud Sam	Gauri	रा, स, नी स, गी रा, म गी रा, स, म, प, धा धा प, धा, प, म, गी रा स	p	रा धा	गी and धा left in Arohi
	Aud Kha	Jogiyá	स रा म. प धा, म, म रा स, स म प धा, रा स, नी धा प धा म, म रा स	u	स म	गो left out altogether and नी in Arohi,

4 Asawari	Sam Sam	Sindhu Bhairavi	प गा री गा, स री ना स, धा प, धा स, ना धा प प	u	स प or गा ना	
	Do	Adáná	म प सं, धा ना, सं, धा ना प, म प, गा म री स	u	स प	Kanra portion isin Purvanga
	Sam Kha	Darbari Kanhra	ना स, री, म प, धा ना सं, री सं, ना प, गा गा, म, री स	p	री प	
	Aud Sam	Asavari	री, म प, ना धा, प, धा सं, ना धा, प, म प, गा री स	u	धा गा	
5 Kafi	Sam Sam	Kafi	ना स, री गा, म प, धी ना सं, सं ना धी, प, म गा, री स	p	प स	
	Kha Sam	Bàgeshwari	स, ना धी ना स, म प गा म धी ना धी, म गा री स	p	म स	प left out in Arohi
	Do	Shahana	ना धी प, म प, सं, ना प म प गा म, प गा, म, री स	u	प स	धी left out in Arohi

Names of Janaka melas	Murchhana	Names of the tunes	Sargams of the tunes.	Purvanga or Uttaranga	Vadi and Samvadi.	Remarks.
	Kha Kha	Megha	री म, रा स, ना प नी स, री म री. प, ना, प नी स, ना प, री म री स	u	स प	धी left out गा used sparingly,
	Aud Sam	Sindhvi or Sindura	स री, म, री, म प, धी. म, प धी री स, स ना धी प म गा री म गा, गा री स	p	स प or धी री	गा and ना left out in Arohi
	Do	Dhanáshri	ना स, गा म प, धो प, ना धी प, गा, प गा, री स	p	प स	री and धी left in Arohi
	Do.	Bhimapalási	ना स म, गा स, प, ना स, ना धो प म, गा री स	p	म स	Do

	Do	Baiwa	स री म प धी प, धी म प, नी सं, सं ना, धी प, धी म, गा री, गा, स	n	स प	गा and री left out in Arohi
	Aud kha	Sàranga	स, री म री, प मी प, धी प म री, म प, नी सं, रीं नो सं, ना प म री स	n	री प	गा left out and धी in Arohi
	Aud Aud	Dhàni	ना स गा म प, ना सं, सं ना प, म गा स	p	गा ना	री and धी left out
6 Khammach	Sam Sam	Jhinjhoti	धी स, री म गो, प, म गी, री स, गो धी प	p	गा धी	
	Kha Sam	Khammach	री स, नी स, गी म प, नी सं, सं ना धो, म प, धो म गो	p	गी नी	री left out in Arohana
	Aud Sam	Desha	री, म प, ना धीप, प धी प म, गी री गो, स	n	प री	
	Kha Sam	Tilaka Kamoda	प नी स री गी, स, री, प म गी, स, री गी, स, नी	p	री प	धो left out in Arohana ना sparingly used

Name of Janaka melas.	Murchhana	Names of the tunes.	Sargams of the tunes,	Purvanga or Uttaranga	Vadi and Samvadi	Remarks.
	Aud kha	Soratha	म री, म प, नी, स॑, स॑ नी धी, म प, धी म री .	p	री धी	गी left out altogether, and धी in Arohana only.
7 Bilàvala	Sam Sam	Bilavala	स धी प म गी, म, री स, स॑ गी, री गी प, नी स॑, री॑, स॑ नी, धी प, म गी	u	स प	म weak in Arohana, धी री, also taken as Vadi Samvadi sometimes.
	Do	Mánda	स, स॑, धी, म, म प, नी, प धी, स॑, म, म प म, धी, प म, म प गी, री स, गी स	u	स म	The time is Vakra throughout,

	Kha Sam	Alahia	गो, री, गी प, धी नी स, स नीं धी, ना धीप, म गी, म री, स	u	धी गी	म left out in Arohana
	Khà Khà	Shankari or Shankurà bharana	सं नी प, नी धी, सं, नी प गी प, गी स प नी स, गी प, नी धी स	u	गी नी	म left out and री very sparingly used in Avarohana only
	Aud Sam	Bihàga	नी स, गी म प, गो म गी, री स, गी म प नी सं, नी धी प, गीं म, गी नी स	u	गो नी	री and धी left out in Arohana and sparingly used in Avarohana
	Aud Aud	Deshakara	सं, धी प, गी प धी स, री सं धी, धी प गी प, गी री स	u	धी री	म and नी left out
8 Todi	Sam Sam	Todi	धा री स रा गा, रा, स, मी प, धा प, मीगा, रा स	u	धा गा	

Names of Janaka melas	Murchhana	Name of the tunes,	Sargams of the tunes	Purvanga or Uttaranga	Vadi and Samvadi.	Remarks
	Aud Sam	Multàni .	नी स, मी गा, प मी धा प, नी स, नी धा प, मी, प गा, रा स	p	नी मी	रा धा left out in Arohana प and स are given as Vadi Samvadi in books, but *see* Chapter X, in this connection.
2. Pùrvi	Sam Sam	Púrvi ...	नी, स रा गी, म गी, मी प, धा प, मी गी, म गी, रा स	p	गो नी	

	Sam Sam	Parja	स, नी धा प, मी प धा, प, गी म गी, रा स नी स, गी मी प, धा नी स	u	स प	रा weak in Arohana
	Kha Sam	Basanta	नी स, मी गी, मी धा स, रा नी धा, प, मी गी, रा स	n	रा मी	*See* Chapter X, प left out in Arohana
	And Sam	Shrirá a	स रा, स मी प, धा प, नी स, नी धा प, मी गा रा स	p	रा मी	*See* Chapter VIII, गा and धा left out in Arohana
10 Màravá	Khá khá	Purija	गी नी रा स, नी धी नी, मी गी, मी धी रा स, मी गा, रा स	p	गी मी	प left out
	Do	Panchama	मा धी, स नी धी, मी धी, मी गी, मी गी, रा स, स म, गी, मी धी, नी धी, नी मी धी	n	मी नी	प left ou

Names of Janaka melas	Murchhana	Names of tunes.	Sargams of the tunes	Purvanga or Uttaranga	Vadi and Samvadi.	Remarks
	Kha Kha	Sohini	गी, मी धी, नी सं, रीं सं, नी धी, नी सं, गीं रीं सं, नी धी, नी धी मी गी	u	धी गी	प left out
11. Kalyani or Kalyana.	Sam Sam	Iman ..	नी धी, प, मी गी मी, प, मी गी, री गी, प मी गी, री, नी री, स	p	गी नी	
	Do.	Iman Kalyana	नी धी, प, मी प, गी, गी मरी, गी री, गी प, गी री स, नी स, धी नी स, री, गी, री गी प, गी री स	p	गी नी	Both Madhyams used.

11 Kalyani —*continued*	Sam Sam	Hamira	स री स, गो म धी, नी धी सं, नी धी, प, मी, प धी प, गी म री स	p	प स or धी री	Both Madhyams used
	Do	Kidara	स, म, प, धी प, म, री स म प मी प, धी प म गी म, री स री स, सं धी सं री सं नी धी प म, प धी प, म री स	p	स म	*Do*
	Do	Gauda Sa ranga	गो, री, री स, गी री, म गी प प मी प, धी, प म गी, री, म गी, प, री स	p	गी धा	Do
	Do	Chhaya Nata	धी प री गो म, प, म गी स रो स स, धो, प, री, गी म प, गी म री स	p	री प	
	Aud Aud	Bhupâli	गी, री, स धी, स री गो, प गी धी प गी, री स	p	गी धी	मी and नी left out
	Do	Hindola	गी स धी मो धी स गी मी धी नी धी, मी गी स	n	गी धी	री and प left out altogether ant नी in Arohana

Names of Janaka Melas	Murchhana	Names of the tunes.	Sargams of the tunes.	Purvranga or Uttaranga p or u.	Vadi and Samvadi.	Remarks.
12. Mixed melas.	Sam Sam	Pilu	नी, स. (गा, री स, नी रा, री स, नीं धा प), नी स, गा म प, गा म गा, री स ( )	p	गा धा	
	Do	Jaijaivanti	रीं गा री स, ना धी प, री. गी म प, म. री गा रीं, नी स	p	री प	Both gandharas and Nishads used.
	Do	Khata	स नी स म गा म, प, पा धा स ना धा प, म गा म, ना धा प, म गा, रा स	u	धा गा	Both रि, ध, ग and नि are used in this raga.
	Do	Ghárá ...	धी नी स, री, गी, म, गी री गी, स नी स, नो री स, धी नी धी, प म गीं, म प धीं, स, नी स	p	री धी	Both Gandharas and Nishads used

The Sargams given above show how the tunes differ from each other It is however unavoidable that portions of different tunes should coincide In cases of these portions being prominent ones, the tunes are said to be containing the others, or made up of two or more tunes Indian music masters analysed a lot of tunes and endeavoured to find out their component tunes It is however difficult to follow them, and more often than not they differ in their opinions, probably because the common points considered were different by different men The tunes also perhaps got altered as time went on It is not of much use therefore to note all these down here Only a few of the common tunes are noted below by way of illustration

Statement showing the analysis of tunes —

Name of tunes	Component tunes			Remarks
	Raga mala Hindi written in 1796	Matla ul-ulum Persian, written in 1847	Sarmaya i Ishrat Urdu written in 1874	
Shuddha Kalyana	Tilaka Gaud and Kamoda	Gond Kamod and Lanka	—	

Names of tunes.	Component tunes			Remarks
	Raga mála Hindi, written in 1798	Matla-ul ulúm Persian, written in 1847	Sarmaya-i-Ishrat, Urdu, written in 1874	
Biláva1a ...	—	Kalyàna and Kidàrà.	—	
Kídára ...	—	Kukubha. Púrvi and Biláva1a	—	
Kukubha ..	-	Bilavala, Purvi, Kedarà and Deogiri	—	
Iman ...	Kedia, Kalyana, and Bilavala.	Kidara Kalyana, and Bilavala	—	
Hamira ...	Kidara Kalyana, and Iman.	Kidara. Kalyana, and Iman.	—	
Shankarábharana.	K dara and Bi avala	Kidara and Bilavala.	Kidara and Bilavala	
Sháma Kalyana	—	—	Kidara and Shuddhanata	

Names of tunes	Component tunes.			Remarks
	Raga Mala. Hindi written in 1798	Matla ul olum Persian written in 1847	Sarmaya i Ishrat Urdu written in 1874	
Malakosha	—	Hindola Basanta Jhinjhoti and Panchama	Purvi, Sham Kalyan and Todi	
Hindola	—	Bilavali Lalita Panchama Puria and Bhairava	Mangala, Vibhasa, and Barari	
Bhairava	—	Hindola Shudha nata Kanbra and Puria		
Shri raga	—	Badhansa Tanka and Gauri	Badhansa Tanka and Gauri, also Kalyana Gujri and Deshkara	
Megha	—	Kalyana Kamoda and Savanta (Sa range and Malar)		

Names of tunes	Component tunes.			Remarks.
	Raga Mala, Hindi written in 1798.	Matle-ul ulum, Persian, written in 1847.	Sarmaya-i-Ishrat, Urdu written in 1874.	
Gauri ...	—	Jhinjhoti, Asavari, Gujari Soratha, Bilavala and Gonda	Shriraga, Rama kali and Gujari	
Kamoda ..	—	Bilavala and Gonda,	Bilavala and Gauri	
Saranga	Devagiri and Malara	Devagiri and Malara,	Natanarayana, Shankarabharana and Bilavala,	
Gauda Saranga.	Saranga and Todi,	Saranga and Gauri or Saranga and Gaurá [Gauri—Nata—Tribeni]	Malakosh and Tribeni	
Sindhavi or Sindhura	Asavari and Ahiri.	Asavari and Ahiri.		
Soratha .	Bhairava, Panchama, Gujari, Bengali and Gandhara	Bhairava, Panchama, Gujari, Bengali and Gandhara.		

Names of tunes	Component tunes			Remark
	Iaga Mala Hindi written in 1794	Matla ul ulum Persian written in 1847	Sarmaya i Ishrat Urdu written in 1874	
Adana	Ahiri (Deshakari and Gujari) Kanhra	Malar and Kanhra	Kanhra Deo akh and Dhanashri	

From a study of the above table it will be clear that the idea of analysing the tunes was to find out the coinciding points out of the different tunes, and not, as is mentioned in several books, that the tunes were really composed by combining two are more tunes as noted The tunes particularly composed by combining two or more tunes bear names showing the composition, e g, Iman and Bilavalacombine and form Imani Bilavala, Iman and Bilavala and Shuddha Kalyana form iman Kalyana, Nata and Bilavala form Nata Bilavala Jaitashri and Shuddha Kalyana form Jaita Kalyana, and so on

Chapter XIV

HARMONY

Ragas and their Raginis of the old writers in harmony with each other. Repudiation of the theory that Indian Music had no harmony. Method of forming Concert Music.

IN the previous chapter it was mentioned that the old writers, Bharata, Hanumat, etc., had divided some of the tunes of their time into several groups of rágas, rágınis, their sons [called putras, पुत्र=son] and daughters-in-law (called Bháryàs भार्या=wife, i.e., of the sons). *Sangita Ratnakara* and several other standard works written after it do not take notice of these groups, and the present tendency is to discard the system altogether, without, it is regrettable, any investigation as to the purpose which the eminent music-makers had in view in this grouping. It will be shown in this chapter that the grouping was not without meaning, and that the several ragas mentioned were in harmony with their raginis, forming what has been described in Chapter XII as Anyonya Laya. The grouping differs to a certain extent among the different writers, of whom there are four

1 Someshwara or God Shiva, the originator of music in India, had, it is said, six ragas, *viz*, Shrí, Vasanta Panchama, Bhairava, Megha and and Natanárayana with six raginis and eight putras to each

2 Bharata, the author of *Natyashastra* is also said to have had six ragas, three of which were different from those of Someshwara They were Bhairava, Malakosha, Hindola, Dípaka Shrí, and Megha each of which had five raginis, eight putras and eight bhárjas

3 Kallinatha takes the six ragas of Someshwara, with six raginis and eight putras to each, his raginis being different from those of Someshwara

4 Hanumat or Hanwanta has the same six ragas as Bharata but his raginis (also five to each raga) are different He has also eight putras, but no Bharyas

The change in the names and connections of the tunes show how the Indian music has undergone considerable alterations The first three systems, *viz*, Someshwara, Bharata and Kallinatha, are now long obsolete For the fourth or the Hanumat system, it is said that the present-day Indian music follows that system This is however questioned by some of the present-day writers, not on very good grounds though. That there have been certain changes is natural and undoubted, but there is not much to show that the ragas etc. of Hanumat school were very different from those used now. The Hindi book *Ragamala* of Gangadhara, written in 1798, takes the rágas and ráginís of Hanumat school, and at the same time seems to be paying homage to Tánasen, which shows that the famous grand musician represented the Hanumat School. As Tánasen's ragas are still taken as standard in Hindustani music, it is not incorrect to assume that the present Hindustani music follows the Hanumat School generally.

The six ragas with their raginis and a few putras of the Hanumat School are noted below:

(1) Bhairava. Raginis—Bhairaví, Sindhaví Bangalí, Barátí, and Madhumádhaví—Putras Purià, Panchama.

(2) Málakosha or Kaushika. Raginis—Todi, Khambávatí, Gaurí, Gunakalí and Kukubha. Putras—Badhansa, Maru.

(3) Hindola Raginis—Bilavalí, Lalita, Rama kalí, Devasakha, and Patmanjarí Putras—Vibhása, Gaurí

(4) Dipaka Raginis—Kanhrá, Kamodi, Deshi, Kidara and Nata

(5) Shri Raginis—Basanta, Dhaná shri, Malashrí, Asavarí and Maravá Putras—Sindhu Gonda, Sankara, Bihagra

(6) Megha Raginis—Tanka, Gujarí, Malár Bhupalí and Deshakara Putras—Saranga, Kalyana, Sobána

Let us now see if as mentioned above the ragas are in harmony with their raginis

Taking the raga Bhairava and its ragini Baratí or Barari the sargama of the latter is (मी रा गा रा स प प नी धी प प गी गी रा स स रा गी रा स) To this sargama let us fit in the samvadis and anuvadis of the different notes having of course in view, as far as possible, to introduce the notes of the raga Bhairava We find the notes (रा रा स धा नी स स गी रा स स रा स धा धा प म गी रा स) which make up a perfect sargama of Bhairava fit in exactly as shown below —

Sargama of Barari	मी रा गी रा स	प प नी नी प	प जी गी सं स	स रा गी रा स
Harmonising tune, Bhairava.	रा रा स धा नी	स स गी रा स	स रा स धा धा	प स गी रा स
Relations of notes in shruti interval.	9/13 0/22 7/15 9/13 2/20	9/13 9/13 9/13 7/15 9/13	9/13 9/13 7/15 9/13 7/15	9/13 7/15 0/22 0/22 0/22
Concord or discord.	Concord (9/13 0/22 7/15 9/13) Discord (2/20)	Concord.	Concord.	Concord.

A few more sargamas of the ragas with those of their raginis are noted down below to show the harmony The sargamas have necessarily to be adjusted, so as to give an equal number of notes to the two tunes in each pair, neither of course losing its specific arrangement of the notes

---

Málakosha and Kukubha.

Sargama of Kukubha	स	स	री	प	म	प	स̅	स̅	प	ना धी	प	धी म	म गी	म गी	स री	स
Harmonising tune, 'Malakosha.'	म	धा	ना	स̅	स̅	ना	धा	म	गा	म	गा	स	ना	स	गा	म
Relations of notes in shruti intervals.	9/13	7/15	7/15	9/13	9/13	6/16	7/15	9/13	7/15	8/14	7/15	9/13	10/12	9/13	6/16	9/13
Concord or discord.	Concord.									Discord.	Concord.		Discord.	Concord.		

Hindola and Bilávala

Sargama of Bilavala	सं सं धी धी प	गी म री स स	स गी री गो प	सं धी म नी सं नी प गी
Harmonising tune, Hindola	गी स धी मी धो	स गी मी धी सं	सं नी धी मी गो	मी गो स स स
Relations of notes in shruti intervals	7/15 0/22 0/22 6/16 4/18	7/15 2/20 7/15 5/17 0/22	0/22 9/13 9/13 4/18 6/16	9/13 7/15 0/22 9/13 9/13
Concord or discord	Concord (7/15 0/22 0/22 6/16) Discord (4/18)	Concord Discord Concord Discord; Concord (0/22 — with 0/22 9/13 9/13)	Concord (0/22 9/13 9/13) Discord (4/18)	Concord (6/16 — with 9/13 7/15 0/22 9/13 9/13)

Megha and Deshakára.

Sargama of Deshakara.	स धी धी स स री	गी प प धी प प	धी धी प प धी प	गी गी प गी री स
Harmonising tune, 'Megha.'	स री री म म री	स ना प री (म) री स	री स नी स री (री) म	प (म) प ना प नी स
Relation of notes in shrutis intervals	0/22 9/13 9/13 9/13 9/13 0/22	7/15 6/16 0/22 9/13 9/13 9/13	9/13 5/17 7/15 9/13 9/13 9/13	6/16 6/16 6/16 6/16 6/16 0/22
Concord or discord.	Concord.	Concord.	Concord (9/13); Discord (5/17); Concord.	Concord.

From the above it will be amply clear that the grouping of the ragas and raginis by the ancient music makers was meant to provide tunes that could be played together as in a concert It enables us to compose concert music, by pointing out the direction in which to proceed to get harmonising or melodious tunes, as such tunes will generally be found within the family An example may be useful

The following is the Sargama of a song in the tune Shankara, sung in Bilavala mela, for which a harmonising tune is required Shankará belongs to the Shri group, so a tune is sure to be found in that group Let us select Ásávari for the purpose Acting on this datum and with the help of the table showing the relations of the notes in Ch VIII, the tune shown below the given tune can be easily formed

Tune 'Shankara.'	स̄	स̄	नी	प	नी	धी	स	नी̄	प	प	गी	प	गी	गी	स	स
Harmonising tune, 'Asavari,'	म प	गी	री	स	री	म	प	प	ना	धा	प	प	धा	स	ना धा	प
Relations of notes in shruti intervals	9/13	7/15	6/16	9/13	6/16	8/14	9/13	7/15	6/16	2/20	6/16	0/22	8/14	7/15	7/15	9/13
Concord or discord.	Concord—					Discord.	Concord.			Discord.	Concord.		Discord.	Concord.		

This ingenious grouping finally repudiates the statement made by some Europeans and Indians that Indian music had no harmony That the art was neglected for some reason or other, and by this time has been altogether forgotten, cannot be gainsaid The above also proves incidentally that the present day Hindustani music follows the Hanumat school for if the ragas and raginis had under gone any considerable alterations they would no more have been in harmony as we find them

CHAPTER XV.

TIME OF RAGAS.

Time determined by the physical and mental condition of the singer. Tivra Madhyama the chief determining note, List of tunes according to time of singing.

IN chapter X it was said that a rága to be attractive must be sung at a time when it pleases the mind, *i.e.*, when its tune or import is in conformity with the state of mind of the singer, or the hearers, or both. The Indian music-masters have fixed times of the day for all the rágas (raginis are included in the word). Opinions differ in a few cases, but not widely. It is intended in this chapter to investigate the principles which govern the problem of time for the different tunes. Here we enter in a way to deal with the relation of mind and music.

The following three things have to be considered in this connection :—

(1) The general inclination of the singer to sing and of the hearers to hear, *i.e.*, what strain they are capable of bearing physically at any particular time.

(2) The general mental condition of the singers and hearers, *ie*, whether happy and composed, or worried and in anxiety

(3) The particular emotion that has to be expressed by the singer or desired to be engendered in the audience

The last, or expression of sentiments, can not evidently be confined to any particular time, and no time can be fixed for ragas when they are meant to express emotions Time can be fixed for them on the first two considerations only

For the first, the day and night may be divided into four periods, *viz*, daybreak to mid day, mid-day to evening, evening to midnight, and midnight to day break Of these, mid-day to evening is the period when a man feels most tired and sluggish and can bear the least strain On the other hand, from midnight to morning one feels the most brisk and smart and, unless troubled by sleep, can exert one's self much better than in any other period The other two periods are midway between them, morning to mid day being perhaps a bit better than from evening to midnight

Now as regards strain in singing, the komala or flat swaras are easier than tívra ones, also the púrvànga (स to म) easier than the uttaránga (प to स̄). Hence it may be taken as a rough general rule that the purvànga rágas with komala swaras should be sung in the period mid-day to evening; púrvánga rágas with tívra swaras from evening to midnight; uttarángaràgas with tívra swaras from midnight to day-break; and uttaránga rágas with Komala swaras from the daybreak to mid-day. For the same reason, ragas sung in Tárasthána are more pleasing after midnight.

The above rough rule is mentioned in other words as that in the first part of the night purvànga notes are more pleasing, while in the latter part the uttaranga ones are better, and that the order is reversed in the day-time. This of course does not take account of the tívra and komala swaras.

To proceed on the second consideration, it is necessary to consider the daily routine in old days of an average Indian, in fair health and having no extraordinary troubles. He woke up at about 4 o'clock in the morning, said his prayers, then getting up and taking his bath performed his worship. After this he went out to work for his living and came back at about mid-day for his meals. After perhaps a little nap he went out again to earn his living, from which he returned rather fagged at about sunset After ablutions he had his sandhya prayers and, taking the evening meals, was free to have a chat with friends or members of the family He went to sleep at about midnight, to get up again before dawn

It will be seen that the hours when he was worried most were the afternoon hours when he had to work for his living, probably hard There was a little worry (not so much as in the afternoon) in the morning also for the same cause Also there must be some in the early morning hours before finally waking up

This found expression in music by the use frequent or otherwise, of tivra madhyama (मँ) This note, having good affinity with many of the other notes, both komals and tivra, is next in importance only to Shadja (स), but being 11 shrutis from it has an almost opposite effect, its anuvadis being vivadis of shadja and *vice versa* While therefore shadja sounds composure and peace, tivra madhyama sounds excitement and worry, hence its use as mentioned Also as one cannot pass on from worry to composure without going through intermediate stages, so the elimination of मँ is done gradually, so that while the note itself is left out, its samvadis and anuvadis are kept on, which are in turn gradually replaced Sometimes, as in the case of Kalyaní mela komala madhyama (म) is introduced along with मी, and the latter is ultimately left out.

The following list gives the janaka melas in the order of their association with tivra madhyama :—

Number.	Janaka melas	मी	Samvadis of मी	Anuvadis of मी
1	Máravá	मी	रा नी	धी
2 and 3	Todì and Pùravì.	मी	रा नी	—
4	Bhairava	—	रा नी	—
5	Kalyánaì *	मी	नी	री धी
6	Bilávala	—	नी	री ध
7	Bhairaví	—	रा	—
8 and 9.	Kàfi and Khammách.	—	—	री धा
10	Asávarí	—	—	री

* In Kalyani, मी is rather sparingly used, hence its position below Bhairava.

The natural order of the Janaka melas to be used during the course of a whole day and night will therefore be something like what is shown on the following circle where the shaded portion indicates the periods of worry

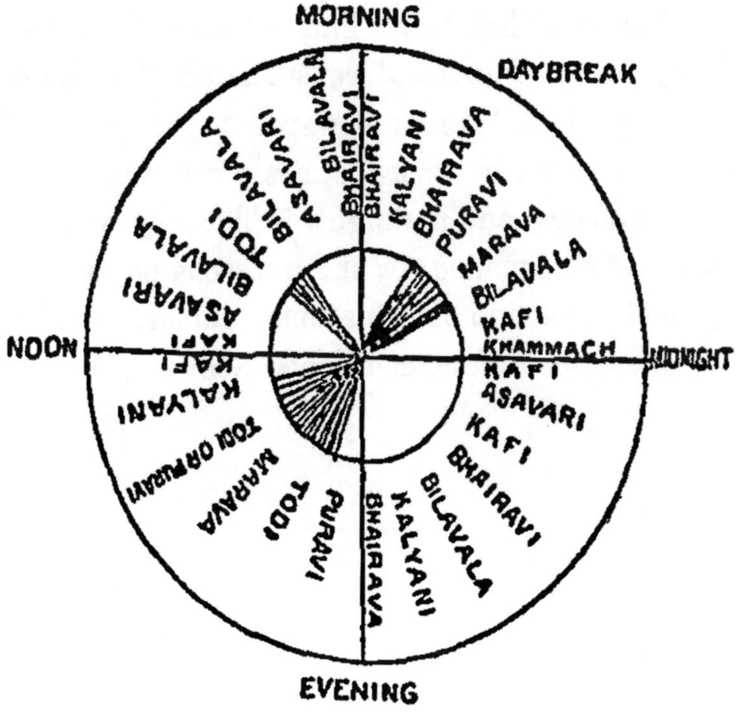

This is very nearly the case in actual prac tice It will be seen that the Janaka mela which starts the abandonment of सा is Bhairava, which has komala rishabha and dhaivata, and tívra gandhara and nisháda, i e two samvadis, and two vivadis of सा This combination of notes, i e

सा गी धा नी, does therefore indicate Sandhiprakásha rágas [Sandhi संधी=junction, *i.e.* of मी and स or, as it happens at the time of night and day].

Similarly, the approach towards मी from the influence of स starts with the mela Káfi which has Komala gándhára and nishâda, and tívra rishabha and dhaivata. This combination (री गा धी ना) being rather a reversal of the above (the Sandhi one) or as it were at the pitch of the swing rightly occurs almost mid-way, *i.e.* at about mid-day and midnight. The intermediate timing is determined by the interchange of the notes of these two combinations, consistent with the positions of मी as mentioned above.

The following is a list of rágas and ráginis with the time prescribed for them —

Time	Names of the tune	Janaka mela
Dawn to early morning	Bhairava	Bhairava
	Rama Kali	
	Vibhása	
	Hindola	Kalyani
	Malkosha	Bhairavi
	Bhairavi	
Earlier part of the morning	Deshkara	Bilavala
	Khata	Asavari etc
	Gunkali	Bilavala
	Bilavala	
	Alahiya	
	Bangali	
Latter part of the morning	Todi	Todi
	Gujari	
	Jaunpuri	Asavari
	Devagiri	Bilavala
	Asavari	Asavari
	Gandhari	Do
	Deshi	Do
Mid day	Suhá	Kafi
	Sughrai	Do
	Sáranga	Do
	Brindabani Sáranga	Do
	Madhumadha	Do
	Gauda Saranga	Kalyani

Time.	Names of the tunes	Janaka mela
Earlier part of afternoon.	Bhimpalásí	Kafi
	Dhání	Do.
	Dhanáshri	Do
	Malashri	Kalyani
	Jaitashri	Purvi
Latter part of afternoon.	Multání	Todi
	Barárí	Marava
	Púriá	Do
	Máravá	Do.
	Shri rága	Purvi
	Purvi	Do.
Evening, dusk	Gauri	Purvi or Bhairava
Earlier part of evening	Kámoda	Kalyani
	Iman	Kalyani
	Iman Kalyana	Do.
	Bhupali	Do.
	Shuddha Kalyana	Do.
	Shama Kalyana	Do.
	Gauda Sáranga	Do.
	Hamíra	Do,
	Chháyánata	Do.
Latter part of the evening,	Kidárà	Do.
	Natanaráyana	Bilavala
	Khammách	Khammach
	Ghára	Do.
	Sindura	Kafi
	Jhinjhoti	Khammach

Time	Names of the tunes	Janaka Mela
Latter part of the evening	Káfi	Kafi
	Darbári Kanhra	Asavari
	Bageshri	Kafi
	Husaini	
	Naiki	
	Tilanga	Khammach
	Tilika Kanoda	
	Shahaná	Kafi
	Adaná	Asavari
Midnight.	Malar	Khammach
	Mian ki Malar	Kafi
	Megha	
	Nata	Khammach
	Gonda	
	Soratha	
	Desha	
	Jaijaivanti	
After midnight	Barvá	Kafi
	Mand	Bilávala
Late after mid night	Shankará	Bilávala
	Bihaga	
	Kukubha	
	Maligaura	Marava
	Bhikara	
	Sohini	
	Panchama	
	Basanta	Purvi
	Parja	
	Kalingra	Bhairava
	Lalita	
	Jogia	
No time fixed	Pilu	Kafi

12

Chapter XVI.

EXPRESSION.

Inner meanings of notes Well-investigated by old writers. Expression of each Shruti note indicated by its name

WE come now to the psychological study of music, to know its effect on the mind. For this it is necessary to investigate the inner meanings of the notes, and how by suitable combinations they can be made to express the desired feelings and generate the desired emotions. The subject was well-investigated by the ancient Indian music-makers like Bharata; the impression created by each musical note was determined, and the feeling each tune gave expression to was specified. This was later on done by personifying the tune, and picturing them with particular feelings or emotions. After the time of Sharngdeva, however, the matter was entirely neglected. Although, as already mentioned in Chapter XIII, some of the books copied out the old description of the personified tunes, the real object was lost. The beautiful description of the rágas (tunes with masculine names) and ráginís (tunes with feminine names) were considered mere poetic imagery, without any real meaning, and it is most likely that additions and alterations were made to original descriptions Music as a fine art almost ceased to be cultivated in India

Except perhaps in a very small circle this state of things still obtains Of the small circle, I may mention Mr H P Krishna Rao (Head master of the Mysore Institute for the Deaf, Mute, and the Blind), who has tried in his book "Psychology of Music", to work out the inner meanings of the notes I have, however, to note with the greatest regret that, like so many other English educated Indians, Mr Rao, a great admirer as he is of the Indian music and its psychological effect, discards all the old carefully worked out notions on the subject, evidently without giving them the proper study they deserved He does not find any use for the shrutis and deprecates the idea of 22 shrutis, and in the matter of inner meanings of notes denounces the old writers Bharata and Sharngdeva as ignorant of the properties, physical as well as æsthetic, of even the fundamental note स [Sa] We have seen that for the correct study of Indian music, shrutis are indispensable and their deprecation does only show an ignorance of the sub ject. Similarly, without studying their works, to call the ancient music-makers as ignorant of the properties of the fundamental note is simply intolerable.

Mr. Rao's indictment of these writers is based on a single shloka (श्लोक verse) giving the chief notes used in the expression of different sentiments. The shloka is as follows :

सरी वीरेऽद्भुते रौद्रे गो बीभत्से भयानके ।
करुणे च धनी कार्यौ हास श्रिंगारयोर्मपौ ॥

It means—In the sentiments expressing heroism and marvellousness, स and रि used ; in anger, ग ; in sentiments exciting disgust, fear and pity, ध and नि ; and in those of humour and love, म and प are used. In the printed edition of Sangita Ratnákara, ध has been shown in place of ग, and *vice versa* which seems to be a copying mistake

Mr. Rao's first objection is that it is impossible that a musical note can express the ascribed emotion by itself but the shloka does not say this, Mr Rao's interpretation of the shloka that the notes by themselves express the several sentiments is not correct.

Another objection of Mr. Rao's is based on the supposition that the emotions expressed by a note and its samvadi must agree with each other So he says that with the emotions mentioned in the shloka स and प can never agree as valour and love are unlike emotions Apart from the fact that valour and love are not antagonistic to each other, his very premise that samvadis must agree in their expressions is wrong He forgets that each note has two samvadis, and his supposition will lead to the absurd conclusion that स agrees with प प with रि, रि with ध, ध with ग ग with नि and नि with स, or that all the notes must express the same sentiment. He actually comes to the conclusion that without embellishments music can express only one sentiment, that of tenderness growing by degrees to pain, and this is not at all surprising with the mistaken supposition

The Sanskrita words Víra, Shringàra, Hása, etc, expressing the sentiments cannot also be very well interpreted by single English words For instance, Vira cannot be interpreted by merely heroism or valour, or shringra by sexual love It is clear therefore that the defect lies not with the author of the shloka, but in the incorrect interpretation of it and wrong suppositions As will be seen later, the use of the several notes recommended by the shloka was determined by a careful analysis of their sounds.

Mr. Rao, with his imposed limitations, takes it that स and प are tranquil notes, रा and धा indicate disturbance, री and धी indicate perception, गा and ना disagreeableness गी and नी enquiry, म optimism or egoism, and मी degradation. On this basis he interprets the emotions expressed by a few of the tunes. The result does not seem to be correct, at least in the case of 'Bhupali,' which according to him is a tune having no sorrow or pain, but which as we know is just the reverse in expression. The defect lies not in the method of interpretation but in the values taken for the several notes.

In European music the tonic (स) is taken to be the firm or strong note, the second (री) the rousing note, the third (गी) the calm or peaceful note, the fourth (म) the solemn or awe-inspiring note, the fifth (प) the clear or trumpet note, the sixth (ध) the sad or melancholy note, and the seventh (नी) the piercing note.

The above meanings given to the notes, by the tonic solfaists, for the European music, or Mr. Rao for the Indian music, are too general and rather vague to be of much use in the interpretation of tunes, or the composition of music to express particular emotions. These certainly require closer investigation of the details and and niceties of sound

The old Indian music makers realised this They did not consider it enough to fix values, by some arbitrary method, merely for the seven notes or some of their modifications, but carefully weighed sounds at shorter intervals *viz*, of one shruti For this purpose, Vinas were constructed with twenty two strings which were tuned to the twenty two shrutis to facilitate comparison The inner meaning which the sound of each shruti indicated was determined in reference to the main note स, which being the natural note uttered without any exertion, represented a state of mind, peaceful and generous, and free from perturbation or extraneous influences

The result thus obtained has been preserved in the newer names of the shrutis themselves, which new names have meanings indicated by their sounds The following is a list of the shrutis, commencing from Chhandovati, on which the chief note स has been fixed with their meanings and derivation of the names —

Chhandovati —from Chhandas (छन्दस्)=free will, independent conduct—indicates peace of mind, independence, heroism, generosity

Dayávati: from Daya (दया) = compassion, sympathy,—indicates pity, sympathy, tenderness, affection.

Ranjani: from Ranjan (रंजन) = colour, pleasing,—indicates pleasure, delight, appreciation.

Raktika: from Rakti (रक्ति) = pleasingness, attachment,—indicates charm, marvellousness, devotion, appreciation, state of getting impassioned.

Raudri: from Raudra (रौद्र) = heat, wrath,—indicates heat, warmth, enthusiasm, anger.

Krodhi: from Krodha (क्रोध) = anger,—indicates anger, cursing.

Vajrika: from Vajra (वज्र) = steel, –indicates severe language, abusing, cursing.

Prasárini: from Prasarana (प्रसारण) = expanding, diffusing,—indicates enquiry, explanation.

Príti: (प्रीतिः) means and indicates joy, happiness, satisfaction, favour, affection.

Márjani: Márjana (मार्जन) = cleaning, purifying, effacing,—indicates clearing one's breast, affection, joking, ridicule, egoism.

Kshiti: from Kshi (क्षि) = to decay, to rule—indicates egoism, complaint of loss.

Rakta from Ranj (रञ्ज्)= to be coloured or attached, to be affected or excited—indicates attachment, devotion, excitement, worry

Sandípini Sandipana (सन्दीपन) = in flaming, kindling, exciting—indicates kindling of the flames of love, excitement due to same

Áláḿpini from Lap (लप्)= to talk—indicates conversation or talk between lovers, expressions of love, affection, entreaty, sympathy

Madanti from Mada (मद), indicates ardent passion, affection, intoxication, madness, sexual love, arrogance, anger due to jealousy

Rohini from Ruh (रुह्)= to grow—indicates development of pleasure, pain, or other feelings. The word also means a girl just grown up, and indicates hopes and fears of early life, solitary musings

Ramya from Ram (रम्)= to rest, to remain quiet—indicates quiet, solitude, musings, apathy, carelessness towards outward show

Ugra (उग्र)= powerful, formidable, sharp—sharpens feelings, also expresses formidableness awe, fear

Kshobhini from Kshubh (क्षुभ्)= to tremble, to be agitated—indicates disturbance, agitation, trembling, unnervedness, pitiableness, extreme worry

Tivrà: (तीव्रा) means and indicates sharpness, acuteness, violence, heat.

Kumudvati : from Kumud (कुमुद्)= unfriendly ; indicates unkindness, criticism, complaint, enmity, avarice. Kumud also means a lotus or water-lily and the shruti may express inward pleasure.

Mandá : from manda (मंद)=slow, apathetic, cold—indicates idleness, inaction, apathy, want of pleasure or enthusiasm.

These twenty-two shrutis were divided by the old music-makers into five categories, known as (1) Díptá (दीप्ता), expressing excitement or stimulation ; (2) Ayatá (आयता). showing diffusiveness, prolixity or expansion ; (3) Karuná (करुणा), expressing compassion and pity ; (4) Mridu (मृदु), showing tenderness of feeling ; (5) Madhyá (मध्या). being neutral and giving expression to feelings not included in the first four. The shrutis coming under each of these categories are as under :—

Diptà :—Tívrá, Raudrí, Vajriká, Ugrá.

Áyatá —Kumudvati, Krodhi, Prasárini, Sandípini, Rohini

Karuná :—Dayávati, Alápini, Madanti.

Mridu.—Mandá, Raktiká, Príti, Kshiti.

Madhyá:—Chhandovati, Ranjani, Márjini, Raktá, Ramyá, Kshobhini.

With this analysis of sounds at small intervals it would be easier to find out what sentiment each tune gives expression to or which tune should be used to express a particular feeling

Before coming to this, however, it is necessary to have a clear idea of the several sentiments and the feelings they produce in the mind This will be dealt with briefly in the next chapter

CHAPTER XVII.

SENTIMENTS OR RASAS.

Rasas defined. Feelings and sentiments classified. How feelings manifest themselves, physically and mentally.

IN this chapter it is intended to describe the different sentiments and feelings recognised in the Indian rhetorics and poetry, and to explain briefly how they are produced or affected. The word for feeling or the state of mind at any time is Bháva (भाव) from the root भू= to be, to exist. Distinction is made between a lasting feeling, or that which pervades the mind during the time under consideration, and those which are transitory, being excited by circumstances and then subsiding. The former is known as a Stháí bhava (स्थाइन्=enduring, permament from स्था to stand). The latter are called Vyabhichàrí bhávas [व्यभिचारिन् =irregular, unfaithful].

The condition or circumstance which alters the existing one or excites a particular state of mind or body is called Vibháva [विभाव]. The sudden appearance of a poisonous snake, or somebody's sudden calling out that there was a snake, which will generate the feeling of fear is Vibhava Meeting or hearing about one's beloved or recollection of sweet old memories about him or her, which may excite the feeling of love is Vibhava Vibháva is of two kinds, Alambana and Uddípana The former (आलम्बन=supporting) is that (person or thing) with reference to which a sentiment arises, the latter (उद्दीपन= exciting) represents the causes which enhance its depth In the case, for instance, of the feeling of sorrow over the death of somebody, the person dead is the Alambana of the sentiment, and the attending circumstances which aggravate sorrow are its Uddípana Vibhávas Alambana or Uddípana may happen in three ways *viz*, Darshana *i e*, by seeing Shravana or by hearing, and Smarana or by recollection, as in the examples cited above

When a feeling is excited in the mind, it usually finds manifestation in some part of the body The symptoms which thus indicate the feeling outwardly are called Anubhavas Palpitation of the heart or drying of the mouth due to the feeling of fear is Anubháva The pleasure expressed on the face of the lovers when they meet and the sadness when they long to meet but cannot, are Anubhavas of the feeling of love

The different feelings or bhávas excited by the appropriate Vibhávas and accompanied by their Anubhávas give rise to what are called Rasas. Rasas (रस) which means taste, essence or sentiment is a comprehensive term for an aggregate resultant emotion. Rasaprabodha (रस प्रबोध), a Hindi book written by S. Ghulam Nabi of Bilgram in 1741 A.D., describes Rasa in a very fine simile. It says: The human mind is the soil where Rasa has got its seeds; Stháibháva is the sprout which irrigated with the water of Vibháva grows into a plant called Anubháva according to the environments Vyabhichárí-bhávas are the flowers, blossoming at frequent intervals and in consonance with the Stháí. These combined produce the honey called Rasa, which is collected by the poet acting as a bee.

The task of the artist lies in depicting the particular Rasas, *i.e.*, giving expression in his work to the sentiments desired to be expressed. The poet (including an orater) does it by means of suitable words with proper accents; the painter and the sculptor by their pictures and sculpture expressing the particular sentiments, and the musician by combining suitable notes to form appropriate tunes. It is clear the poet has the greatest advantage; the painter and the sculptor come next as they get the advantage of the Anubhavas which have been determined for each bhava or sentiment The task of the musician is rather difficult, but if he can combine poetry with music in his songs and take help of the Anubhavas in his gesticulations, his performance will surely surpass that of the others Hence the necessity of suitable songs for music and the utility of proper gesticulating

The feelings which give rise to sentiments are grouped into nine, enumerated in the following shloka of Sáhitya Darpana

रतिर्हासश्च शोकश्च क्रोधोत्साहौ भय तथा
जुगुप्सा विस्मयश्चेत्थमष्टौ प्रोक्त शमोऽपिच ॥

i e, (1) Rati (रति)=pleasure, amusement, love, affection, sexual pleasure or passion, (2) Hasa (हास)=laughter, merriment, ridicule, (3) Shoka (शोक)=sorrow, grief, pitiableness (4) Krodha (क्रोध)=anger, wrath, (5) Utsaha (उत्साह)=effort, determination, perseverance, firmness, fortitude, (6) Bhaya (भय)=fear alarm, terror, (7) Jugupsa (जुगुप्सा)=censure, dislike disgust (8) Vismaya (विस्मय)=wonder, surprise, admiration, and (9) Shama (शम)=tranquility, rest, absence of passion, restraint of senses The last has been put in the shloka as if outside the category, because it is in fact absence of a real feeling It has not been recognised by Bharata, the author of *Natyashastra*, as a feeling giving rise to a sentiment.

The Rasas (रसाः) which arise from the above feelings or bhávas are respectively known as (1) Shringára (शृंगार), (2) Hása (3) Karuna (करुण= sorrow). (4) Raudra (रौद्र=wrathful, terrible), (5) Víra (वीर), (6) Bhayanaka (भयानक=terror), (7) Bibhatsa (बीभत्स=disgust), (8) Adbhuta (अद्भुत= marvellous), and (9) Shanta (शान्त=undisturbed) The last as said above, is not recognised in the *Natyashastra* On the other hand, there are other writers who recognise two extra rasas, Vátsalya (वात्सल्य) or affection, especially for one's offspring, and Bhakti (भक्ति) or worship and devotion. These are surely included in Shringára, Vira, Adbhuta, and Shánti.

Shringára, the sentiment of love, is so called because it is the most important of the rasas [from shringa शृंग=peak of a mountain]. It is also therefore known as Rasarája. It is of two kinds, *viz.*, (1) Sambhoga Shringára (संभोग), when the lovers enjoy each other's company, and (2) Vipralambha Shringára (विप्रलंभ) when there is separation due to any cause.

Víra, which is the sentiment of heroism is fourfold, *viz*, (1) Dána Víra (दान), *i.e.*, heroism based on liberality or the sentiment of enthusiastic liberality (2) Dharma Víra (धर्म) i e., heroism based on piety and righteousness, or the sentiment of enthusiastic piety, (3) Daya Vira (दया), i e heroism based on compassion, or the sentiment of chivalrous compassion, and (4) Yuddha Vira (युद्ध) or heroism in battle

No further comments are needed in respect of the other rasas

The nine bhavas noted above are Sthai when they are the pervading feelings of a particular Rasa, but when they come and go strengthening the pervading feeling, they are Vyabhichari The latter are known as (1) Tanu Vyabhichari when affecting the body (तनु=body) and giving rise to Anubhavas, and (2) Mana Vyabhichári when affecting the mind [मनस्=mind]

The former manifests itself in eight ways, viz (1) Sweda (स्वेद)= sweating, (2) Stambha (स्तम्भ) = motionlessness (3) Romancha (रोमांच)=horripilation or erection of hair (4) Swara bhanga (स्वरभंग)= broken articulation, (5) Kampa (कंप) = trembling, (6) Vivarna (विवर्ण)= change of colour (7) Ashru (अश्रु)= tears, and (8) Pralapa (प्रलाप)=prattling talking nonsense Jrimbha (जृम्भा) or yawning is also included in this by some

The latter (Mana Vyabhichari) has thirty three manifestations, viz, (1) Nirveda (निर्वेद)= in-

13

difference to worldly objects, self-humiliation; (2) Gláni (ग्लानि)= exhaustion, fatigue; (3) Shanká (शंका)= fear, misgiving; (4) Alasya (आलस्य = want of energy; (5) Asuyá (असूया)=envy, jealousy; (6) Shrama (श्रम)= exertion, weariness; (7) Mada (मद)= conceit; (8) Dainya (दैन्य)= miserable state, low-spiritedness; (9) Chintà (चिन्ता) = anxiety; (10) Moha (मोह)= perplexity; (11) Smiriti (स्मृति)= recollection; (12) Dhriti (धृति)= contentment, (13) Vrídà (व्रीडा)= shame, bashfulness; (14) Harsha (हर्ष)= joy; (15) Chapalata (चपलता)= swiftness, fickleness, unsteadiness; (16) Jadatá (जडता)= dullness; (17) Garva (गर्व)= pride, arrogance, (18) Vishàda (विषाद)= disappointment; (19) Avega (आवेग)= agitation, flurry; (20) Utkantha (उत्कंठा)= longing for a beloved person or thing; (21) Nidrá (निद्रा)= sleepiness; (22) Swapna (स्वप्न)= dreaming; (23) Apasmára (अपस्मार)= epilepsy (this manifests itself more as a tanu vyabhichári); (24) Avahitthà (अवहित्था) = concealment of an inward feeling; (25) Amarsha (अमर्ष)=anger due to disrespect etc., intolerance; (26) Ugratá (उग्रता)=ferociousness; (27) Vyádhi (व्याधि)=ailment, sickness; (28) Mati (मति)=under standing; (29) Unmàda (उन्माद)= madness; (30) Marana (मरण)=death due to extreme grief, shame or fear; (31) Vibodha

(विबोध)=becoming conscious, (32) Tràsa (त्रास)=fear, alarm, and (33) Vitarka (वितर्क)=reasoning, doubt

Each of these bhávas has its particular vibhávas and physical manifestations, but to mention all these is beyond the scope of this book Only the rasas with their sthái bhávas are repeated in the statement below, which also gives the connected vyabhichárıs, both bodily and mental

---

Statement showing the Rasas with their Bhavas.

No.	Names of Rasas.	Bhávas.	Connected anubhávas or Tanu Vyabhicharis.	Connected Mana Vyabhicharis.
1	Shringára	Rati		
	(1) Sambhoga		Sweda, Stambha, Romancha, Ashru	Gláni, Mada, Dhriti, Harsha, Chapalata, Garva, Ávega, Nidrá, Unmáda.
	(2) Vipralambha.		Sweda, Stambha, Swarabhanga, Vivarna, Ashru, Pralapa.	Nirveda, Shanka, Alasya, Asúyá Shrama, Mada, Dainya, Chintá, Smriti, Jadatà, Vishádа, Avega, Utkanthá, Nidrá, Swipna, Avahitthá, Amarsha, Vyádhi, Unmada, Marana, Trása, Vitarka
2	Hása.	Hasa	Vivarna, Hása, Swara bhanga.	Mada, Smriti, Harsha, Chapalata Garva, Avega, Mati, Vitarka.
3	Karuna.	Shoka	Sweda, Stambha, Swarabhanga, Vivarna, Ashrn.	Shankà, Alasya, Asúyà, Shrama, Dainya, Chinta, Smriti, Vrídá, Vishádа, Utkanthá, Swapna, Avahitthá, Vyádhi, Marana, Trasa.

4	Raudra	Krodha	Sweda Románcha Swara bhanga Kampa Vivarna, Pralapa	Asuyá Mada, Smriti Garva, Avega, Amarsha, Ugratà Unmàda
5	Vira	Utsáha	Sweda Romàncha Vivarna Ashru,	Mada Smriti, Dhriti Harsha Garva, Avega Amarsha Ugratá Mati, Vibodha, Vitarka
6	Bhayánaka	Bhaya	Sweda Stambha Romancha Swara bhanga Kampa Vivarna Ashru Pralapa	Shankà Shrama Dainya Chintá Smriti Vrida, Vishada, Avega, Apasmara, Irása
7	Bíbhatsa	Jugupsá	Románcha, Praláp a	Mada, Garva Avega Amarsha, Ugratá Vyádhi
8	Adbhuta	Vismaya.	Sweda Stambha Románcha Swara bhanga Kampa, Vivarna	Asuyá Dainya, Chinta, Harsha, Jadata, Avega Mati
9	Shánta	Shama	Stambha Románcha, Swara bhanga, Ashru	Nirveda Dainya Smriti Dhriti Harsha Utkantha, Nidra, Mati, Vibodha.

CHAPTER XVIII.

EXPRESSON.

Value of the notes in connection with different sentiments. The use of Vadi, Samvadi and Vivadi notes. Importance of Nyasa Jati ragas

KNOWING the different sentiments and the way they find expression as explained briefly in the previous chapter, and the expression given by each Shruti, as shown in the chapter preceding, it would be easy to assign values to each of the notes in the matter of expression, as also to their combinations in the different tunes. An endeavour will be made in this and the following chapters to do this. Let us in the first instance see if the shloka, giving the chief notes for the different Rasas (sentiments), quoted in Chapter XVI, and to which an exception has been taken by Mr. Rao, conforms with the analysis.

According to the old writers (Sharngdeva and others) Shadja comprises the shrutis Manda, Chandovàti, Dayavati, and Ranjani. These clearly indicate Vira Rasa, so sa (स) is correctly noted as being the chief note of that sentiment. Rishabha takes Raktiká and Raudrí, and is not incorrectly taken as the note for Adbhuta Rasa Gandhara comprises Krodhí Vajrika and Prasáriní and aptly indicates Raudra or sentiment of anger Madhyama and Panchama extend over Príti, Marjaní Kshiti, Rakta Sandipini and Alapiní, and hence these two notes take up the sentiments Hása and Shringára Madantí, Rohiní Ramyá, Ugrá Kshobhiní Tivra, and Kumudvatí go to Dhaivata and Nishada which have therefore been correctly mentioned as being used in Bíbhatsa Bhayanaka and Karuna rasas It will thus be seen that the ancient music makers did not fix any haphazard values to the notes, but fixed them in a most scientific way

With the old Indian music, comprising 19 notes, most of the emotions could be expressed What could not be done was accomplished by the expert singers by lowering or raising their voices in smaller intervals than provided by the notes In stringed instruments, like Vína and Sitár, this was done by stretching the string or wire over the frets to produce a sharper note This is called Míd and known as quarter half etc, according to the sharpness required, the full Míd giving the next higher note

The present day music having a smaller number of notes—only 12 against the 19 of the old music—can express the sentiments very partially, and the musician must strive much harder to produce the real effect The reduction in the number of notes has in this respect been to our great disadvantage, and has perhaps largely contributed to the disappearance of the science of expression, comprising the old Arthádhyáya, from Indian music.

The twelve notes of the present-day Indian music are fixed at the shrutis noted against them and can in a composition express the emotions indicated by the shrutis, unless the notes are sharpened or flattened: स—Chhandovati, रा—Ranjani, री—Raudni, गा—Vajriká, गी—Prasárini, म—Márjani, मी—Raktá, प—Álapini, धा—Rohiní, धी—Ugrá, ना—Tívrá, and नी—Kumudvati.

The twelve notes of the harmonium which, as has been noticed before, have equalised intervals, represent very nearly the same shrutis as above, excepting that गा is nearer Krodhi than Vajriká, and ना nearer Kshobhini than Tívrá. Here no Míḍ is possible and intermediate sounds are attempted by sounding two adjacent notes closely following each other with short-intervalled repetitions. It cannot however produce the correct note wanted, although the effect is pleasing.

This is also done in Sitár and is known as Zamzamá or Gitkirí.

The following list of the nine rasas gives chief notes of the present Indian music, which are approximately appropriate for each rasa, according to the value of the shrutis given by the old writers, the Mid noted being half

1 Víra — स, स with Mid, रा, म, प

2 Adbhuta — स, रा, रा with Mid, री

3 Raudra — री, री with Mid, गा, गी

4 Hása — स, गा, गी with Mid, म, म with Mid

5 Shringára — स, गी गी with Mid, म, मी, मी with Mid प, प with Mid, धा, धा with Mid

6 Bíbhatsa—म with Mid, मी धा with Mid, धी, ना नी,

7 Bhayanaka—मी, धी, धी with Mid, ना, नी

8 Karuna—स, गी, मी, प, धा, धा with Mid, धी, धी with Mid, नी, नी with Mid

9 Shanta—स, स with Mid, रा with Mid, म, मी धा with Mid नी with Mid

The notes as shown above have to be used more frequently than others, as Vadis or Samvádis, and in the form of tanas and Alankáras, so that the particular rasas may be expressed

It will be seen from the list, as also from the shrutis representing the notes, that the notes री, गी, धी, and नी, do each represent two or more different sentiments and with suitable anuvadis are capable of changing the import of a tune meant to be expressed by its Vádi and Samvádi. Hence they have been taken by old writers as taking the roll of Vivádis and, as such, they have to be avoided or cautiously used

To illustrate the difference caused by different Vádi notes, two tunes Deshakára and Bhùpálí may be taken as examples. Both these have the same notes, स री, गी, प and धी, having म and नी left out. Their Sargams are as follows:—

Deshakara—धी, प, गी, प, धी स̅, री̅ स̅, धी प, गी, री, स, with धी and री as Vàdi and Samvádi, respectively.

Bhupali—गी, री, स धी̲, स री गी, प गी, धी प गी, री, स with गी and धी as Vàdi and Samvàdi, respectively.

Now taking the tune Deshakàra, its Vadi धी representing Bíbhatsa and Karuna rasas suggests a feeling of disgust, distress, and fear, while the Samvadi री expresses admiration, which with स brings consolation. प with धी seems to offer an explanation; also its existence and the absence of नी eliminate all bitterness of feeling The tune, therefore, expresses worry and distress over one's shortcomings which cannot it appears, be helped There is a hope from the magnanimity of the addressee, or the person referred to, of pardon, which gives consolation The tune may well be used in a prayer

In the case of Bhupali, गी is Vadi which shows anger, and धी Samvadi showing worry रे and प near गी excite admiration and love and soften down the anger, while स brings calmness Here also there is no bitterness as नी is absent The tune therefore expresses sorrow and anger at the separation, or perhaps the inattention, of one's beloved, but love and admiration get the better of anger and cool it down leaving the lover reconciled to his or her rather pitiable lot

The difference in the import of the two tunes due to the different Vadi notes is apparent It is also worth noticing how in the tune Bhúpálí the sentiment of anger has been alleviated by the use of the note री, which is a Vivádi of the Vadi note गो

The use of necessary notes as Nyasa or Apannáysa, (i e, at the end of a tune or the different parts of it) is also important in the matter of expression, for the note at the end of a tune leaves an impression, which the intermediate notes do not. As noted in Chapter XIII, this is not unfortunately taken into consideration in the present-day music. In the old Indian music, much importance was laid on this point. Tunes were divided into eighteen categories, called Játi rágas, according to their Nyása (note at the end of a tune), and their Vádis, Vivádis, etc., determined. Some of them are given below as examples. The value of the notes meant has been noted in the remarks column in terms of our present notes.

Statement showing some of the old Játi Rágas

No	Name of Játi tune	Nyá note	Ansha or Vadi notes	Apannyas notes	Varjita if any	Remarks as to the value of the notes meant
1	Shádjí	स	स ग म प ध	ग प	नि	Notes as in Kalyáni mela with गी sharpened a shruti
2	Arshabhi	रि	रि ध नि	रि ध नि	स प	Notes as in Khammuah mela with धी and ना flattened
3	Gándhárí	ग	स ग म प नि	स प	रि ध	Notes as in Bhairavi mela using मी for प and ना flattened
4	Rakta, Gándhari	ग	Do	ग	Do	Notes as in Kaliyani mela
5	Madhyamá	म	स रि म प ध	स रि म प ध	ग नि	Do
6	Panchami	प	रि प	रि प नि	ग नि	Do

No	Name of Jàtı tune.	Nyàsa note	Ansha or Vádı notes.	Apannyas notes.	Varjıta, ıf any	Remarks as to the value of the notes meant.
7	Kármáravı	प	रि प ध नि	रि प ध नि	—	Notes as ın Khammach mela with री, धी, and नी, flattened.
8	Dhaıvatí	ध	रि ध	रि म ध	प स	Notes, as ın Bılávala mela.
9	Naısbadí	नि	स ग नि	स ग नि	प स	Do.
10	Kaıshıkı	ग प नि	स ग म प ध नि	स ग म प ध नि	रि ध	Notes as ın Bhairaví mela

Each of these Jati ragas represented, it appears, a certain general sentiment according to the Nyasa which was made specific by the Vádi taken, and the arrangement of other notes, for any tune in the *group*. For instance, *Shádjí* group perhaps stood for Víra rasa and a tune with स as Vádi and omitting ध and नि like Hema Kalyána, would express Yuddha Víra or heroism in battle. Arshabhi group indicated marvellousness, and a tune with रि as Vádi will express appreciation, but with ध as Vadi it will express awe and fear and so on.

Our present tunes have no defined Nyása, and besides, some of the old notes are no more used, hence they cannot very well be classified under the old Játi rágas which would have facilitated their interpretation to a certain extent.

The subject of Jati rágas is at present only of an academic importance and need not be pursued here further. It however indicates the importance of Nyasa in the interpretation of tunes, which is worth looking into by experts when composing tunes for particular sentiments.

We may conclude this chapter after adding that in the matter of expression, the laya of tunes (*see* Chapter XI), and the Sthana and loudness of notes, have also a useful bearing. For subjects of grave and sober nature, for instance, the laya used will be Vilambita, the Sthâna of the notes will be Mandra and Madhya, and the tone mild; while for the subjects expressing love, sport, and merriment, a quicker (druta) laya, and notes in Madhya and Tárasthána will be more suitable. Anger will require a louder tone.

CHAPTER XIX

COMPOSITION AND INTERPRETATION OF TUNES

Method of expressing the several sentiments in Music How tunes could be interpreted, explained by illustrations Why certain tunes can have more than one interpretation

IN this chapter we shall make an endeavour to illustrate how tunes could be found out or formed to express certain ideas, and *vice versa* how certain given tunes might be interpreted

For the former, let us take, as an illustration, the famous soliloquy of Hamlet in Shakespeare's play of that name [Act III, Scene 1] The soliloquy expresses an utter disgust of the world and a great disappointment at the troubles of an outrageous fortune To get rid of them, the Prince considers whether it would be nobler to end his own life or to fight against the troubles and end them The former he dismisses as it was not certain what might happen after death, leaving him determined to take arms against the evils

14

The sentiments expressed are therefore grief, disgust, anger, and determination, giving rise to Karuna, Bibhatsa, Raudra and Vira rasas. Appreciation and love are altogether absent, so Shringára and Adbhuta are excluded. The notes to be used would therefore be Shadja, Gándhára, Madhyama, Dhaivata and Nisháda. Gándhára would be komala, *i.e.*, on the shruti Vajriká. Madhyama would be komala to help Shadja in Virá rasa, as also perhaps tívra, because there is worry. Dhaivata would be komala, the subject being one of solitary musings. Nisháda would also be komala on the shruti Tívra; perhaps it would be better on the previous shruti Kshobhiní. Raudra and Vira are the Sthái rasas, hence the Vádi must be from स, ग and म A tune in the Gándhári group (Jati ragas, pp. 205 and 206) with स, म as Vadi and Samvadi, and रि left out, would be appropriate to the sentiments expressed in the soliloquy. In our present music, the tune *Màlakosha* would approach this very nearly as it has no रि or प, and has its force on स, ग, म. It has of course no सा.

As another illustration, let us take the sentiments of Rishi Vishwámitra when the nymph Mainaká presented to him the baby Shakuntalá, the offspring of their union, as represented in the famous picture "Birth of Shakuntalá" of Ravi Vermá The Rishi is made to recollect how in an unguarded moment he succumbed to the charms of the nymph and lost the fruits of his austere devotion He upbraids and despises himself, hides his face and refuses to look at the child

Here also appreciation and love are altogether absent, and rishabha and panchama have to be excluded The notes to be used are shadja, gándhára, madhyama, dhaivata and nishada There being no valour or Víra rasa, shadja is not to be accompanied by ग, there is only a little determination for not having to do anything with the affair further Chyuta shadja on the shruti Mandá might have done in this case but we have no such shadja The anger being directed against self, it consisted mostly of recitation of the faults and shortcomings rather than of abuses, hence gandhara will be tívra on the shruti Prasárini Madhyama as said cannot be komala, it should be tívra, there being so much worry Dhaivata must also be tivra on the shruti Ugra, it was given komala in the previous example as it was a soliloquy Nishada is also to be tívra on shruti Kumudvatí The emphasis is to be on गी,धी and नी, so the vadi, samvadi and if possible

Náyasa ought to come from these notes. Among the old Jáṭi rágas, the tune will perhaps be from the Naishádi group, with गी, नी as vàdi and samvádi, and प and रि left out. In the current music the tune *Hindola* will be appropriate.

The nymph Mainaká is also not very happy with the result of her union with the Rishi. The child Shakuntalà was a human girl and could not be kept in the land of gods, with apsarás and fairies, and separation was unavoidable. Mainaká's sentiments may be analysed as below :—

1. She is worried over the beautiful human child whom she could not keep with her. She argues within herself the possibility of her father keeping her and also hopes to that effect.

2. She then approaches Vishwámitra, shows love towards him, describing the child appreciatingly, and asks him to keep it with him.

3. On the Rishi refusing to look at the child and to do anything with it, the nymph is greatly disappointed, and there is extreme worry and anger.

4. The girl has to be left to her fate. There must be an abundance of maternal love and extreme grief.

The notes to express these sentiments will be as follows :—

(1) Worry will require the use of नी and मी, the solitary musing and arguments within her own mind mean धा, प, and गी, affection towards the child will need the intercession here and there of म and प, and its loveliness will be indicated by रा, स will be required rather frequently to express hope in the ultimate end of worry The tune *Parja* would appear to express the sentiment very approximately, its sargama being स, नी धा प, मीप, धाप, गीमगी, रास, नीस, गीमीप, धानीस, the vadi being स

(2) Here also the notes will be the same, but गी will be the chief note, and म and प will be more frequently used, as the chief object is enquiry, which is accompanied by the expression of love मी is not required, नी being enough to indicate the inward worry In fact, नी might also be used sparingly The appropriate tune seems to be *Kalingra*, whose Sargama is नी स रा गी म, गी म, प धा, नी धा प, गी म, गी रा स, and Nyasa and Vadi गी

(3) The sentiment expressed here is Karuna mixed with a little anger, the notes being धी, नी, मी, and गी There is no question of love, so प must be left out There will probably be a little, not much, recitation of the girl's loveliness, for which रा will be required The tune fitting in

would be *Sohini* with its Sargama मी धी, नी स, रा स, नी धी नी स, ना धी, गी, and धी गी as Vàdi and Samvadi.

(4) This is Vàtsalya rasa or the expression of maternal love and would require the notes स, रा, म and प. The idea of separation of the child from the mother will need a frequent use of धा on the shruti Rohiní, and of नी on shruti Kumudvatí, to express the extreme worry. धा would be the chief note. It seems *Jagiyà Asávari* will be an appropriate tune, its Sargama being स रा म म प प धा धा स स नी धा प धा धा म प नी प म गी रा with धा, रा, as Vadi and Samvadi

For interpretation of given tunes, the process followed above is to be reversed. This has been done in the previous chapter in interpreting the tunes Deshakára and Bhupali. A tune or two more may be examined :—

(1) *Hamira.*—The sargama of *Hamria* is स री स, गी म धी, नी, धी, स, नी धी, प, मी प धी प, गी म री स, with धी, री, as vádi and samvàdi. स री स indicate enthusiasm and happiness, and गी म धी ridicule and joking. नी धी together would bring in disgust, but प being vivadi of धी and indicating love keeps this sentiment down. With प, मी also indicates devotion and not worry. The tune therefore expresses happiness, merriment, and joy.

(2) *Desha*—The sargama of *Desha* is री, म प, ना धी प, प धी प म, गी री गी, स, with प and री as vádi and samvadi and प as nyása प with री stands for love, appreciation, and devotion, ना and धी on the shrutis Tivra and Ugra, coming in between, simply enhance the sentiment गी on Prasarini indicates explanation and complaint The tune therefore expresses the sentiment of love or Shringara, perhaps Sambhoga, with some complaints of inattention

The import of the tunes can surely be slightly modified by the more or less frequent use of the different notes For the same cause the interpretation of a tune by different experts cannot always coincide exactly Some of the tunes, however, can have more than one interpretation

It is clear that if a tune could be played on two or more Janaka melas having their notes in the same pitch (or in the octave), it will be capable of more than one interpretation according to the notes or shrutis of the respective Janaka melas This is possible only if the Janaka melas are on the same grama Among our present Janaka melas, only Bhairavi and Kalyaní are on the same grama (Madhyama grama), and so the tunes sung or played on these melas are capable of two interpretations As an example, the tune *Hindola*, one interpretation of which has been given at the beginning of this chapter, may be taken.

The notes of Bhairavi Janaka mela are स रा गा म प धा ना स, with shruti intervals of 2, 4, 3, 4, 2, 4, 3. The corresponding notes of the Kalyáni Janaka mela with the same intervals are नी स री गी मी प धी नी, so that with स having the same pitch in the two cases, a tune belonging to one of these melas will be playable on the other by the slight atteration of नी of the latter for स of the former, स for रा, री for गा and so on. The sargama of *Hindola* on the Kalyání scale is गी, स धी, मी धी स, गी, मी धी नी धी, मी गी स.

This, when transferred to Bhairavi, becomes म रा ना पा ना रा, म, प ना स ना, प म रा. स being the same in the two cases, a second interpretation is possible with the notes on the Bhairavi mela. रा ना and म are chief notes, which indicate an occasion of happiness and enthusiasm that may be a unique one. प shows affection towards the object or hero of the occasion. The absence of गा and धा show an absence of anger or misgiving. A great birth or a coronation may well be described in the tune *Hindolo*.

It is not suggested here that the rágas prescribed under the particular Janaka melas need

CHPTER XX.

PERSONIFICATION OF TUNES.

Descriptions of personified Ragas and Raginis.
Meant to express sentiments.
How to Interpret them.

IN Chapters 13 and 16, references were made to the picturesque descriptions, given in several books on music of the different rágas and ráginis, which have been personified. Except in a few cases, the descriptions in the several books do not differ materially. A few are noted below by way of illustration, taken from Rágamálá of Gangádhara and Náda Vinoda of Goswámís Pannálál and Chunnilàl.

Bhairava—a yogì in the form of God Shiva, having three eyes, trishúla (trident) in hand and a garland of human skulls on his neck, engaged in meditation of God. He is wearing white clothes and has bhashma (ashes) rubbed on his forehead. This with the moon in his Jatá (matted hair) doubles his handsomeness.

Bhairaví—a beautiful fair-coloured lady, wearing white Sárí, and red bodice, engaged in worshipping God Shiva on the Kailásh mountain with lotus flowers She is holding Vína in her hands

Bhupálí—a lady, separated from her lover, wearing saffron coloured Sári, and grown pale owing to the fire of separation

Deshakara—a lady with her body bright as gold, her face like the moon, her eyes like lotus, and full of sexual desire, she is playing with her husband

Jogiyá Asavari—a lady with matted hair and her body besmeared with ashes [bhashma] She has Trishúla and bowl in her hands and wears an angry look Also practising Yoga and Vairágya she gets entranced in God

Hamira—A prince, expert in music, sitting in Mahfil [entertainment hall] He is engaged in merriment, and smiling amorously towards his wife thinks of going to bed

Kedára—a lady ascetic with matted hair, serpent in her neck, worshipping God Shiva with rapt attention and Vairagya The tune is also shown as a male with the same ascetic form

Málakosha—a brave warrior sitting amongst warriors He is reddish in colour and has a red stick in his hand, and is wearing a garland made of soldiers' skulls. The R'aga is also represented as a prince of fair colour, wearing blue garments and a necklace of pearls, and holding a white stick in his hand. He is sitting among ladies who all love him.

Deshi—(Desha), a beautiful lady with green clothes, desirous of meeting her husband, whom she is awakening from sleep on different pretexts. As Desha (a rága) the tune is shown as a handsome, 18-year old, cheerful young man, wearing white clothes engaged in music and thinking of meeting his wife.

Parja—a fair-coloured lady, with body bright as gold. She is looking askance or through a corner of the eye. She is an embodiment of Karuna and Shánta rasas.

The descriptions, it is clear, are meant mainly to represent certain sentiments, and comparing them with the expressions of some of the tunes worked out in the previous chapter, the two will be found to be showing almost similar sentiments. The form, in which the sentiments have been expressed is not, however, very convenient, and it is a pity we cannot very well utilise the labours of the old writers An admirable endeavour has been made to this end by my friend L. Kannu

Mal, M A, in his book 'Sahitya Sangita Nirúpana," wherein to interpret the sentiments contained in the descriptions of the personified ragas and rgáinís he takes the aid of the Indian literature on Rasas or sentiments In the particular portion of this subject, known as " Nayaka and Náyiká Bheda ', especially appertaining to Shringara rasa, there is a description of different sorts of men and women, according to the age, habits, temperaments degree and direction of affection etc, and profuse illustrations have been given to show their feelings and sentiments, and how these feelings and sentiments express themselves, *i e*, bhavas and anubhavas To find the expression of a certain raga or rágini it is necessary to determine which particular Náyaka or Nayiká the description of the tune represents, the sentiments and anubhavas can then be easily fixed upon

Let us take Kedara ragini as an example It represents a Nayika or lady who is (*a*) Praudha, or fully grown up, (*b*) Swakiya or fully devoted to her husband, and (*c*) Proshita Bhartrika or Patika, *i e*, whose husband has gone out to another town or country Her worshipping Shiva is to get victory over Kamadeva (Cupid) as the God had killed Kamadeva The description given in the book

"Rasaprabodha" of Praudhà Vipralabdhá or the lady who missed to find her husband at the appointed place, is interesting in this respect. It says, "Seeing the place vacant, the lady bent her head, as if, feeling the full power of Kámadeva, she was entreating God Shiva."

Now the feelings of Swakíyà Praudhá Proshita patiká are expressed in the following terms in "Rasaprabodha"—"In the city of her body separation has come in as a new sort of Kotwal (City Police-officer), so that, after making her keep up the night, Prána or life-vigour has to leave early in the morning for toil in other directions. Although her eyes are raining day and night the source of supply is not diminished; water from the eyes serves as ghee (clarified butter) to the fire burning in the heart." This then is the expression of the rágini Kedárá. It stands for Vipralambha Shringára. [*See* Ch. XVII].

As a male figure the tune will represent Shánta rasa and devotion. So Kedára can be used to express both these rasas. The tune being one belonging to the Janaka mela Kalyání can, we know, have two expressions.

Chapter XXI

GESTICULATING AND DANCING

Practical playing on instruments, acting and dancing beyond the scope of this book Work of an actor and a dancer in connection with music briefly explained

IN chapter I it was noted that Indian music dealt with and divided itself into seven subjects *viz*, (1) Swara or notes, (2) Raga or tunes, (3) Tála or rhythm, (4) playing on instruments, (5) Artha or meaning of the tunes (6) Bháva or gesticulating, *i.e*, acting so as to explain the meaning of the songs and to express the sentiments of the tunes, and (7) Nritya or dancing The subjects 1, 2, 3, and 5, have been dealt with pretty fully in the above pages No 4 or the playing on instruments, No 6 (Bháva) and No 7 (dancing) are subjects mostly practical, and therefore beyond the scope of this work, which deals with theory and principles However, the principles laid down in connection with notes, tunes, their expression and rhythm, are expected to be of substantial help in these subjects as well

Taking the playing of instruments, for instance, the sargams given of the different tunes will enable the player to play those tunes. Knowing the relation of the notes to each other, *i.e.*, the samvádís, anuvadis, and vivádis of the vádi note he will be able to expand the tunes, keeping vívádis out The theory and principles of harmony which make it possible to prepare orchestral music can particularly be utilised in instrumental music only. The several tálas are as essential for the instrumental as for vocal music. Of course, how each instrument, víná, sítár, piano, harmonium, violin, flute, tablá, or other instruments should be played has to be learnt from music-masters or Ustáds, or from the books written for the purpose.

Bháva or gesticulating requires action and posture expressive of the meaning and sentiments of a song. It may be taken for granted that the wording of a song and its tune would be expressing the same feelings. The actor has two duties to perform. He has to explain the important points of the song by the proper motion of his body and hands, as also to indicate the sentiment expressed in the tune, chiefly by means of face, eyes and hands.

In chapter XVII, in which sentiments have been classified, anubhavas or bodily manifestations, as also mental manifestations, of each feeling and sentiment have been noted A real actor has to put them in practice For instance in Bhayánaka rasa, with fear as the chief feeling, the anubhavas are sweating, trembling, tears, etc, and these are to be shown by the actor Sweating and tears, if not real, have to be indicated by hand, wiping the forehead and cheeks The Mana vyabhichárís like shanka, chinta or anxiety etc, are to be expressed in the face and eyes.

Dancing is a combination of Bhava and tala or gesticulating and timing, the latter particularly in a very high degree, as it has to follow the tanas and paranas of tablá and pakhavaja For this reason, the word Tala (ताल) is sometimes taken as a combination of the initial of two words Tandava (ताण्डव) and Lasa (लास) which were the peculiar dances of God Shiva and his consort Parvati, respectively As in showing Bhava, the gestures and postures, assisted by hands and eyes, indicate the meaning of the song and the import of the tune sung The work of a dancer is therefore very difficult and exacting Nardas " Sangíta Makaranda ' gives the following as attributes of a dancer —

15

अंगेनालम्बयेद्गीतं हस्तेनार्थं प्रदर्शयेत् ।
नेत्राभ्यां भावयेद्भावं पादाभ्यां ताल निर्णयः ॥

i.e., by his body he indicates the general import of a song, with his hands he shows its meaning, with his eyes he expresses the feeling and sentiments, and with his feet he keeps the tála and time.

The old books on the science of dancing give the diferent postures expressive of the different sentiments, as also how tálas and their tánas are to be carried out in the dance. How certain things and ideas are to be expressed by hands etc. are also noted. But it is outside the scope of this treatise to go into all these.

CHAPTER XXII

NOTATION

The system of recording music at different times

Advantage of the Indian system of recording notes by their initials

THE desire to preserve for posterity the the experience and knowledge gained, or the result of observations made has been natural for all time This has been the cause of the invention of writing and the alphabet In the case of music too, attempts have all along been made by the music masters to record what they or their predecessors or contemporaries had achieved The notation, as the alphabet of this recording of music is called, has been somewhat different in different times In India, the initials of the names of the notes, *viz* स, रि, ग, etc, have been the basis of this recording from very early times It is not known how the notes were recorded before the present names were adopted

The following are the chief items to be indicated in music writing (1) Notes or swaras, (2), their pitch, *i e*, whether Shuddha or Vikrita, (3) their octave, *i e* whether Mandra, Madhya, or Tárasthána; (4) Sút, in case the notes are meant to be blended together; (5) Andolan or swinging of notes, which in quick succession is called zamzamá; (6) Míd, in stringed instruments, when the wire or string is so much stretched over a fret as to sound another higher note; (7) Tála in case of timed rágas or songs; (8) Rasa or sentiment indicated by a tune, its time of singing, derivation, or any other information that the writer may like to record.

In old days, from the time of Bharata to that of Shàrngdeva, the notes were indicated by their initials (स, रि, ग, etc.) and their pitch by mentioning the particular Múrchhaná which gave the notes of the tune. We know there were seven múrchhanás for each gráma or fourteen for the two gramas in use. At this time, we also know, several of the notes had more than two forms, so mentioning the múrchhaná was the best way to show which notes were meant. The higher octave or Tára sthána was indicated by a small vertical line, and the lower octave or Mandrasthàna by a dot over the initials. Andolan is indicated by using dirgha (long) vowels with initials of the notes [*e. g.*, ध गा मा म म नी स नि.]

Tála was noted down in cases of timed ràgas, as also other items mentioned above in No. 8.

The following description of Rága Kukubha, taken from Sangíta Ratnakara, illustrates the point "Kukubha is derived from Madhyama, Panchami and Dhaivatí Jati ragas, Dhaivata is its Ansha (Vadi), and graha (starting note), Panchama its ending note (Nyasa), the Mùrchha na is Dhaivata Murchhana of Shadja grama, Prasanna Madhya arohí varna is the alankara, Rasa (sentiment) expressed is Karuna, Yama is the presiding god, it is sung in Sharad season"

Then follows the sargam and alapa of the raga

Ragavibodha combined the notes and their pitch, or the swaras and their murchhana values, into one, by giving the shrutís instead of the notes used in a particular tune

Later on, on the introduction of Janaka melas, múrchhanas were replaced by Janaka melas, the notes being given in the usual way by their initials

The books on Sitar gave their own scales or Thaths, and for the notes the number of frets counted either from the top or from the bottom Míd and Zamzama were mentioned where requir ed the latter was sometimes indicated by a small line of dots Sút was also noted by a line above the notes to be blended

In all this notation, however, there was no way to indicate periods of less than one syllable or mátrá. To meet this defect, for some time in recent years, the English system of notation was adopted in some parts of Bengal. This system we know consists of a scale of horizontal lines which with their intermediate spaces indicate the different notes of the gamut for several octaves, and the period each note is to be used for is indicated by the signs representing crotchets, minims, etc. This dealt all right with small periods of less than a mátrá, but it had the following disadvantages:

(1) It caused a muddle in the Tála, chiefly in the different parts of its anga indicated by strokes, as they could not be easily shown, and (2) the peculiarity of the Indian system of indicating the notes by initials of their names was lost. This method of indicating the notes is superior to other systems in that the short names psychologically bring the real notes at once to the mind of the singer, which the mere horizontal lines are incapable of doing. The use of the English system could not therefore last long.

Then came the elaborate and rather cumbrous system introduced by Pandit Vishnu Digambara Pulaskara, in which signs have been fixed for multiples and fractions of mátras [i e, 1/2, 1/4, 1/8, 1/16, 1/3, 1/6 and 1/12] These are to be placed under the swara initials स, रि, ग, etc For pitch of the notes, there are different signs to be placed before the notes to show whether they are shuddha or in a vikrita form However, no signs are given before shuddha notes and those generally used in a Mela (scale), as for instance in tunes on the Bilavala mela, Tivra Madhyama if used will be given its sign, while in those on the Kalyani mela, Shuddha Madhyama will be given one This is not only confusing, but needs mention of the particular Janaka mela used, which if done the several signs become superfluous To show the Sthana (octave), the notation consists of three horizontal columns to take the notes in the three octaves, Tara Madhya and Mandra

The difficulty of Tala, as mentioned above in the case of English system, remained the same in this, to meet which Tala strokes are separately shown by the numbers, 1, 2 and 3, showing the Sama, ordinary strokes and Khali respectively

There is no doubt that an endeavour has been made in this system to include everything in its notation, but being rather cumbersome it cannot, although current, be regarded as a success on the whole

Another system, which started almost simultaneously with that of Pandit Vishnu Digambara and is gaining popularity, is that of Pandit Vishnu Náráyana Bhátkhande. Here Shuddha swaras in Madhyasthána are shown with ordinary initials, Komala Swaras have a hyphen underneath, and Tívra Madhyama a small vertical line above म. Mandrasthana swaras have a dot below, and Tárasthana swaras a dot above, the initials. In the case of Sút a curved line is given over the notes to be blended together.

The method of writing consists of horizontal columns divided by vertical lines, to show the strokes or parts of the anga of the Tála to be used, each stroke or part giving its mátras (two, three, or four) separately. Whether the stroke has a Sama or Khali, or is an ordinary one, is also indicated respectively by signs x, o, and the figures 1, 2, 3. etc. In case a mátrá requires more than one note (swara), all the notes required are written together in the space provided for the mátrá. Fractions of mátrás are thus indicated. The exact fractions 1/4, 1/8, 1/16, etc , it is hardly necessary to show.

Pandit Bhatkhande's system has all that is ordinarily required and is at the same time simple It has however the small defect that it cannot work well in scripts which have dots on their letters *e g*, Urdu or Persian Besides, dots and small hyphens are liable to be ignored in print or in reading So *Muarifun Naghmat*, the excellent Urdu book by Saiyed Nawab Ali Sahib, has added an "a" (ا alif) for Komala swaras and an "i" (ی ye) for Shuddha or tivra ones, the fixed swaras स and प going with the former For Mandra and Tara Sthanas, hyphens are added below and above the notes respectively This is a desirable change and has, with the exception of the fixed notes, been adopted in this book also, *vide* Chapter VII

Printed at The Belvedere Press Allahabad by F Hall

ERRATA.

Page	Line	Insert	Delete	Read	For
vi	26	XIII as No of the Chapter.			
36	16	—	—	in the	is
37	13	—	—	रि	नि
37	17	—	—	and	end
38	9	—	—	Recognises	Recognise
38	25	—	7/16		
40	2	—	—	पण्डिता :	पण्डित :
44	15 and 16	—	and Tivratira Dhaivata		
46	19	—	—	Gandhara	Gandhavra
47	19	—	—	Madhyama	Madhya.
48	9	—	—	Madhyama	Madhyam
50	14	—	—	Ragalapana	Ragalpana
63	9	—	—	Tivra	Tirva
63	7	—	—	or	on
79	7	—	—	अस्तप्राय	अस्वप्राय
82	5	—	are		
87	18	—	—	उडुव	उड्डव

Page	Line	Insert	Delete	Read	For
95	1	7 as first word			
95	10	—	—	Bhairavi	Bharava
109	Last	—	in order		
113	3	Comma after 'was and now	bracket		
126	9	—	—	गागा	गाग
152	22	—	—	Kedara	Kdara
15[illegible]	24	—	—	Bilavala	Biavala
157	[illegible]	—	and		
206	18	—	—	Initials	Initial
225	25	—	—	Narda s	Nardas
226	1	—	—	द्र	द
227	6	—	one the		